READINGS ON

STEPHEN CRANE

OTHER TITLES IN THE GREENHAVEN PRESS LITERARY COMPANION SERIES:

AMERICAN AUTHORS

Maya Angelou
Emily Dickinson
William Faulkner
F. Scott Fitzgerald
Nathaniel Hawthorne
Ernest Hemingway
Herman Melville
Arthur Miller
Eugene O'Neill
Edgar Allan Poe
John Steinbeck
Mark Twain

BRITISH AUTHORS

Jane Austen
Joseph Conrad
Charles Dickens

WORLD AUTHORS

Fyodor Dostoyevsky
Homer
Sophocles

AMERICAN LITERATURE

The Great Gatsby
Of Mice and Men
The Scarlet Letter

BRITISH LITERATURE

Animal Farm
The Canterbury Tales
Lord of the Flies
Romeo and Juliet
Shakespeare: The Comedies
Shakespeare: The Sonnets
Shakespeare: The Tragedies
A Tale of Two Cities

WORLD LITERATURE

Diary of a Young Girl

:N PRESS

mpanion

TO AMERICAN AUTHORS

READINGS ON

STEPHEN CRANE

David Bender, *Publisher*
Bruno Leone, *Executive Editor*
Brenda Stalcup, *Managing Editor*
Bonnie Szumski, *Series Editor*

Bonnie Szumski, *Book Editor*

go, CA

Every effort has been made to trace the owners of copyrighted material. The articles in this volume may have been edited for content, length, and/or reading level. The titles have been changed to enhance the editorial purpose of the Opposing Viewpoints® concept. Those interested in locating the original source will find the complete citation on the first page of each article.

Library of Congress Cataloging-in-Publication Data

Readings on Stephen Crane / Bonnie Szumski, book editor.
        p.   cm. — (Greenhaven Press literary
companion to American authors)
    Includes bibliographical references and index.
    ISBN 1-56510-643-1 (lib. bdg.). —
ISBN 1-56510-642-3 (pbk.)
    1. Crane, Stephen, 1871–1900—Criticism and interpretation. I. Szumski, Bonnie, 1958–   . II. Title: Stephen Crane. III. Series.
PS1449.C85Z82   1998
813'.4—dc21   97-22100

Cover photo: UPI/Corbis–Bettmann

Copyright ©1998 by Greenhaven Press, Inc.
PO Box 289009
San Diego, CA 92198-9009
Printed in the U.S.A.

"You can feel nothing . . . unless you are in that condition yourself."

———Stephen Crane

CONTENTS

less in realism and continuity of thought than in giving an overall mental and physical impression of his characters.

FOREWORD

*"'Tis the good reader that
makes the good book."*

Ralph Waldo Emerson

The story's bare facts are simple: The captain, an old and scarred seafarer, walks with a peg leg made of whale ivory. He relentlessly drives his crew to hunt the world's oceans for the great white whale that crippled him. After a long search, the ship encounters the whale and a fierce battle ensues. Finally the captain drives his harpoon into the whale, but the harpoon line catches the captain about the neck and drags him to his death.

A simple story, a straightforward plot—yet, since the 1851 publication of Herman Melville's *Moby-Dick*, readers and critics have found many meanings in the struggle between Captain Ahab and the whale. To some, the novel is a cautionary tale that depicts how Ahab's obsession with revenge leads to his insanity and death. Others believe that the whale represents the unknowable secrets of the universe and that Ahab is a tragic hero who dares to challenge fate by attempting to discover this knowledge. Perhaps Melville intended Ahab as a criticism of Americans' tendency to become involved in well-intentioned but irrational causes. Or did Melville model Ahab after himself, letting his fictional character express his anger at what he perceived as a cruel and distant god?

Although literary critics disagree over the meaning of *Moby-Dick*, readers do not need to choose one particular interpretation in order to gain an understanding of Melville's novel. Instead, by examining various analyses, they can gain

9

numerous insights into the issues that lie under the surface of the basic plot. Studying the writings of literary critics can also aid readers in making their own assessments of *Moby-Dick* and other literary works and in developing analytical thinking skills.

The Greenhaven Literary Companion Series was created with these goals in mind. Designed for young adults, this unique anthology series provides an engaging and comprehensive introduction to literary analysis and criticism. The essays included in the Literary Companion Series are chosen for their accessibility to a young adult audience and are expertly edited in consideration of both the reading and comprehension levels of this audience. In addition, each essay is introduced by a concise summation that presents the contributing writer's main themes and insights. Every anthology in the Literary Companion Series contains a varied selection of critical essays that cover a wide time span and express diverse views. Wherever possible, primary sources are represented through excerpts from authors' notebooks, letters, and journals and through contemporary criticism.

Each title in the Literary Companion Series pays careful consideration to the historical context of the particular author or literary work. In-depth biographies and detailed chronologies reveal important aspects of authors' lives and emphasize the historical events and social milieu that influenced their writings. To facilitate further research, every anthology includes primary and secondary source bibliographies of articles and/or books selected for their suitability for young adults. These engaging features make the Greenhaven Literary Companion Series ideal for introducing students to literary analysis in the classroom or as a library resource for young adults researching the world's great authors and literature.

Exceptional in its focus on young adults, the Greenhaven Literary Companion Series strives to present literary criticism in a compelling and accessible format. Every title in the series is intended to spark readers' interest in leading American and world authors, to help them broaden their understanding of literature, and to encourage them to formulate their own analyses of the literary works that they read. It is the editors' hope that young adult readers will find these anthologies to be true companions in their study of literature.

INTRODUCTION

During the years he lived in New York's Bowery exploring a life of poverty, Stephen Crane wrote, "You can tell nothing . . . unless you are in that condition yourself," indicating his firm belief that in order to write about something, one first had to live it.

This philosophy, which Crane in fact spent much of his short life pursuing, is supremely ironic for the author who wrote what is perhaps the most well known novel about the Civil War, an event that occurred before he was born.

Crane was bothered by this inconsistency, too, and as a war correspondent desperately sought to go to war, any war—and did, first the Greco-Turkish War and then the Spanish-American War. Only after these experiences did Crane feel confident that *The Red Badge of Courage* was accurate.

Time after time, Crane used events he had personally experienced as fodder for his work, whether it was war, a stranding in an open boat, or a book about women of the Bowery. For one of his works, he even wrote two versions, a nonfiction newspaper article and the short story "The Open Boat."

Whatever he wrote, Crane's work is remarkably accessible. *The Red Badge of Courage, Maggie: A Girl of the Streets,* and his many short stories seem as fresh and straightforward as when they were first written almost a century ago. Although as a journalist Crane's articles were always a bit too literary, a bit too philosophically wide ranging for his "just the facts" editors, as a novelist, these techniques seem deceptively simple and appealing.

Unlike many of his contemporaries, such as Joseph Conrad, Crane's work seems especially suited to the general reader. No complex biblical and literary allusions, no heavily wrought prose or vocabulary, make his work difficult. Yet Crane also dealt with grand themes: Why are some people doomed to poverty? Why is there war? How can one find purpose in one's life? In *Readings on Stephen Crane,* critics discuss such concepts, as well as Crane's techniques and his surprisingly modern style. Many of the articles are by well-known literary figures who personally knew and grew to like Crane and admire his work.

This book contains several helpful features for those new to literary criticism. Each essay's introduction summarizes the article's main ideas and gives a bit of background on the author. Notes explain difficult or unfamiliar words and concepts throughout the book. A chronology lists important dates in the life of the author and presents him in a broader historical context. A bibliography includes works for further research as well as historical works of interest. Finally, an annotated table of contents and thorough index make each volume in the Literary Companion Series a complete research tool in itself as well as a launching point for further exploration.

As readers delve into Crane's life and work, the editor hopes that they will move beyond Crane's best-known works and explore his remarkable poetry, for example, and his darker, moodier pieces such as *George's Mother* and *The Monster.* For, although usually read exclusively by scholars, all of Crane's writing is remarkably fresh, and as he hoped, real.

STEPHEN CRANE: A BIOGRAPHY

An entirely objective account of Stephen Crane's life may be an impossibility. "I cannot help vanishing and disappearing and dissolving," Crane once wrote, and his statement seems especially true as one launches into his biography. The story of his life is often speculative and/or based on secondhand information. Crane's first biographer, Thomas Beer, must be held somewhat responsible for touting his heavily fictionalized biography as fact. It is possible, however, to sort through the least disputed information to forge an accurate rendition of Crane's short life.

Stephen Crane was born in Newark, New Jersey, on November 1, 1871, to Jonathan Townley Crane, a Methodist minister, and Mary Helen Peck Crane, the daughter of a clergyman. Stephen was their fourteenth and last child, though at the time of his birth, only eight of Crane's thirteen siblings had survived childhood. Crane's father named him Stephen after the "ancestor who signed the Declaration," a forefather who, indeed, was an integral part of the revolutionary political process.

Stephen's father had an established parish and a position of some importance in the Methodist Church, but he lost both when he publicly condemned the faith's embrace of the so-called Holiness Movement. Like other denominations at the time, the Methodists encouraged members to experience a rebirth, or spiritual renewal that affirmed their faith. When Crane objected on the grounds that it seemed to diminish members' first conversion, the church made him an itinerant preacher, doomed to travel from church to church throughout New Jersey. The Crane family joined him in these temporary appointments, which included moves to Bloomington and Paterson, New Jersey. Throughout this period, Stephen's mother worked tirelessly for the temperance cause.

Thus Stephen's early childhood was shaped by parents who were educated and civic minded, used to making persuasive speeches, admirers and cultivators of the spoken word. In addition, his older brother Townley became a newspaper columnist and lived at home during Stephen's early childhood. Thus, Stephen was exposed to books and ideas and grew up in a home that was alive with thought, albeit conservative thought. Stephen seems to have absorbed the intellectual atmosphere relatively early. His brother Edmund remembers Stephen as also wanting to write from a very young age:

> When he was about three years old, an older brother, Townley, was a cub reporter on one of the Newark dailies . . . and when writing his stories at home would often call on his Mother for the correct spelling of a word. Stevie was making weird marks on a paper with a lead pencil one day and in the exact tone of one, absorbed in composition, and coming to the surface only for a moment of needed information, called to his mother, "Ma, how do you spell 'O'," this happening to be a letter he had just become acquainted with.

At age eight, Stephen's world changed drastically when his father died of a heart seizure in 1880. His mother suddenly had to support her family, and she became even more involved in her work for the temperance movement. In 1883 the Crane family moved to the Methodist resort of Asbury Park, New Jersey, where Helen Crane was elected president of the Asbury Park and Ocean Grove chapters of the Women's Christian Temperance Union (WCTU). Townley Crane, Stephen's brother, ran a summer news agency near Asbury Park, and Helen Crane contributed reports on religious events. Stephen spent his time riding his pony on the beachfront and developing a passion for baseball.

In September 1885, Stephen enrolled in Pennington Seminary, a Methodist boarding school where for ten years his father had been principal. He did not take to the school, dropping out in December 1887. In the spring of 1888, Crane transferred to Claverack College, a coeducational military academy in upstate New York. Crane called his years at Claverack "the happiest years of my life, although I was not then aware of it." Although still a mediocre student, Crane played baseball, fell in love with a young woman named Jennie Pierce, and earned the rank of first lieutenant, in charge of his own company of students. A recollection of Crane's years at Claverack was recorded much later by a fellow student, Harvey Wickham. Wickham's account, tinged with resentment, notes that Crane talked of "poker and baseball," and that "all his life he strove to win recognition as a regular fellow . . . and he failed. Only women and hero worshipers ever really liked him."

For reasons that are unknown, Crane transferred to Lafayette College in Easton, Pennsylvania, in 1890 to study mining and engineering. Pledged to Delta Upsilon fraternity, a story survives of Crane's hazing, a tradition for every young would-be fraternity man. Ernest Smith, one of the hazers, recalled that after breaking down Stephen's door,

> An oil lamp burning in the room indicated plainly . . . the figure of Crane backed into a corner with a revolver in hand. He was ghastly white . . . and extremely nervous. There was no time to escape what might have proved a real tragedy until Crane unexpectedly seemed to wilt limply in place and the loaded revolver dropped harmlessly to the floor.

Crane failed five of his seven courses in his first semester at Lafayette, and promptly transferred to Syracuse University, which was cofounded by his mother's uncle, Jesse Peck. Crane seems to have fit in a bit better there, playing both catcher and shortstop on the college baseball team. He also wrote for the school paper and published his first short story, "The King's Favor," in the *University Herald*. Still, the discipline of school life must have left Stephen cold, because he determined to quit school in June 1891. Recalling Syracuse, Stephen wrote:

> I did little work at school, but confined my abilities, such as they were to the diamond. Not that I disliked books, but the cut-and-dried curriculum of the college did not appeal to me. Humanity was a much more interested study. . . . When I ought to have been studying my next day's lessons I was watching the trains roll in and out of Central Station.

During the summer of 1890, Crane worked with his brother Townley on his newspaper service and took a camping trip with friends to Port Jervis. Most scholars believe the trip, which lasted a few weeks, was the inspiration for his "Sullivan County Sketches." In June 1891, Crane left for New York City, establishing a permanent residence with his brother Edmund, who lived in Lake View, New York. Living with Edmund seems to have been a stabilizing force, a respectable base from which Crane explored the slums of New York City and a safe haven to which he returned. During this year his mother died, and Crane, at the age of twenty, became an orphan.

For the next few years, Crane pursued a vagabond life in

the city, supporting himself in no conceivable way. He seems to have earned very little, living in dormitories with artistic and medical student friends and acquaintances, and thriving on researching urban life. The winters of 1892–1893 and 1893–1894 were particularly brutal, and Crane's hobo lifestyle took a toll on his health. Most scholars agree that in these years he contracted the tuberculosis that plagued him throughout his life. Indeed, it seems that Crane felt a need to not only experience the city, but experience its worst aspects. To write a sketch in 1894 called "Experiment in Misery," Crane dressed as a tramp and spent the night in a flophouse because "you can tell nothing . . . unless you are in that condition yourself."

In the summer of 1892, Crane returned to Asbury Park to work with Townley. He reported the mundane events of the tourist town, including the visits of well-known people. One assignment, a parade, should have been just as routine, but Crane's spin on it resulted in his dismissal from the agency and, indeed, ruined the agency's reputation.

His subject was the annual parade of the Junior Order of United American Mechanics. Crane's opinionated, stylish article called the parade "the most awkward, ungainly, uncut and uncarved procession that ever raised clouds of dust on sun-beaten streets." He went on to criticize the spectators and Asbury Park itself as a town filled with idle tourists who created nothing. The piece offended everyone, and the paper had to reprint a retraction. Crane returned to New York City.

Crane resumed a hobo's life in the Bowery, all the while at work on his first great novel about the slums of New York, *Maggie: A Girl of the Streets.* In *Maggie,* Crane uses his experience of Bowery life to describe a young girl, beaten down by poverty and trapped into prostitution, who becomes pregnant and takes her own life. Crane self-published the book in 1893 and sent a copy to William Dean Howells, a writer known for his realistic style. The book received little attention, and Crane recalled that the public reception of *Maggie* was "My first great disappointment. . . . Nobody seemed to notice it or care for it." William Dean Howells, however, did like it, and invited Crane to tea. Howells offered to help Crane place *Maggie* with a publisher, but, even with his influence, he was unable to obtain a publisher—most were uninterested in the controversial character as well as the unknown author.

Buoyed by Howells's encouragement, however, Crane refused to give up. Now living with a painter friend, Corwin Knapp Linson, Crane settled in to write what would become *The Red Badge of Courage*. He read books on the Civil War, but grew frustrated by the dull and emotionless way the men who had participated in the conflict described their experiences. "I wonder that *some* of these fellows don't tell how they *felt* in those scraps! They spout eternally of what they *did* but they are as emotionless as rocks!" From this quote, it is clear that Crane hoped to do the opposite with his book— to paint a picture of the war from Henry Fleming's emotions and feelings. Indeed, while reading the book it is difficult to follow any of the battle events or troop movements, as the reader experiences the war through Henry's confusion, fear, and attempts to cover for both. The book remains one of the most memorable war novels ever written.

Around the time Crane finished *The Red Badge of Courage*, he began to write poetry. Some scholars speculate that Crane's poems, similar in length and technique to the poems of Emily Dickinson, were inspired by a reading of her work by Howells, but others call such an incident fictional. Crane's poems are far less ambiguous than Dickinson's, though they are just as moving and focus on grand themes. Although Howells was also impressed with Crane's poems, no publisher would touch them. Yet Crane was able to place some stories during this time and begin a slow climb out of poverty.

After *The Red Badge of Courage* sat at a publisher's for six months, Crane took it back and sold it in serial form to a newspaper syndicate, where it was to run in papers in Philadelphia, New York, and California. *The Black Riders*, his first collection of poems, was also accepted for publication, and he began to attract a small readership.

Meanwhile, in January 1895, Irving Bacheller, the owner of the newspaper syndicate that published *The Red Badge of Courage* in serial form, sent Crane on a tour of the West to send back stories as a roving correspondent. In that capacity he met fellow author Willa Cather, whose report of their meeting foreshadowed much:

> Crane was moody most of the time, his health was bad and he seemed profoundly discouraged.... He went about with the tense, preoccupied air of a man who is brooding over some impending disaster.... I am convinced that when I met

him he had a vague premonition of the shortness of his working day. . . . He stood a dark and silent figure, somber as Poe himself.

At the time, Crane was on his way to Mexico for Bacheller to continue his western sketches. Crane sent back a number of stories, entitled "Mexican Sights and Street Scenes," that were published in the newspapers in tandem with segments of *The Red Badge Of Courage*, which had by this time gained widespread popularity and made Crane a much-in-demand writer. The Mexico stories were wide ranging, focusing on individuals, places, and lifestyles, including his encounter with a group of *bandidos* who threatened to rob him.

In May 1895, Crane returned from Mexico after hearing that *The Black Riders* had been published. Critical response to the poems was mainly confusion—most critics, while pointing out similarities to Dickinson, were baffled. The poems remain Crane's least well known works. Though Crane was disappointed in the reviews, he was surprised and pleased to find that *The Red Badge of Courage* had met with success.

Crane spent the summer with his brother in Hartwood, New York, writing *The Third Violet* and going horseback riding. "My idea of happiness is the saddle of a good-riding horse," he wrote. *The Red Badge of Courage* was published in book form in October 1895, and was well received, especially in Great Britain. In fact, the book received a glowing review in London by a critic who called it "one of the deathless books which must be read by everybody who desires to be, or to seem, a connoisseur of fiction." Crane was surprised and disconcerted by the sudden success and attention the review brought him both in Britain and, after publication there, in the United States. He feared that he might not be able to write meaningful work without experiencing hardship himself.

During this time, Crane tentatively courted, through correspondence, Nellie Crouse, a society belle. Their correspondence, from January through May 1896, is fraught with earnestness on Crane's side and cool flirtation on Crouse's. The two had met once and only once before Crane went to Mexico. While the potential love affair never gained momentum, the correspondence reveals much about Crane's thoughts of being worthy of fame and the title of gentleman.

In the fall of 1896, Crane was living in New York and had

decided to do a series of stories on the police and the magistrate's court in the rough Tenderloin district. The series was published in William Randolph Hearst's New York *Journal*. Crane began his efforts while Theodore Roosevelt, police commissioner of New York, was working to clean up corruption in the police force. As a reporter, Crane became involved in a scandal that gained him widespread repute. Because of Hearst's taste for "yellow journalism," or making up and/or sometimes making news, many scholars suspect that Crane had a hand in staging the events.

Crane met two chorus girls on September 15, in order to "know more of that throng of unfortunates . . . [to] study the police court victims in their haunts." The three were joined by Dora Clark, a friend of the women. Crane left to take one of the girls to a cable car, and returned to find police arresting the other two for soliciting. He offered to testify that Dora and the other woman were with him; in court the next day, the judge dismissed the case and reprimanded the arresting officer. Crane had just made himself a target of the New York Police Department.

Dora did not let the matter drop, however, and pressed charges against the arresting officer. During the subsequent trial, in which Crane once again testified, he was grilled endlessly about his associations and portrayed as an immoral philanderer. The arresting officer was acquitted. Rumors circulated that after the trial Crane was harassed to the point that he left New York. Whether it was harassment or simply the fact that sometime in November he signed on as a Cuban correspondent for Bacheller is not known. Bacheller paid him seven hundred dollars to write stories about the Cuban nationalist uprising and Crane left for Jacksonville, Florida. While he waited for a ship to take him to Cuba, he met Cora Taylor, the madam of a house of ill repute known as the Hotel de Dream. (Some scholars take issue with the term *madam*, as Cora's establishment provided a place of assignation only, and the prostitutes did not live on the premises.) Crane began to live at the Hotel de Dream and he and Cora developed a close relationship.

Crane finally found a ship—he signed on as a crewman aboard the *Commodore*, a vessel transporting illegal guns to the Cuban rebels. The boat left for Cuba on New Year's Eve 1896, but sank on the open sea, and Crane found himself aboard one of three lifeboats, fifteen miles from land. About the experience, Crane wrote two stories, an account for the New York *Press* and his famous short story, "The Open Boat." Crane, like his short story's protagonist, survived, and he returned to Cora. Still frustrated in his attempts to get to Cuba, Crane signed on with Hearst to report on the Greco-Turkish War. Cora decided to follow him, assuming the pseudonym Imogene Carter and the title of the first woman war correspondent. Crane started out on the side of the Greeks, but quickly became disenchanted with the entire endeavor. He wrote, "You can repeat to yourself, if you like, the various stated causes of war, and mouth them over and try to apply them to the situation, but . . . the mind returns to the wonder of why so many people will put themselves to the most incredible labor and inconvenience and danger for the sake of this—this ending of a few lives." Crane's purpose was more than the thirteen stories he wrote for the *Press*, however. He hoped to confirm, and through letters he claimed to have done so, the accuracy of *The Red Badge of Courage* as a war novel. After his short stint in the war, in June 1897, Crane moved to Surrey, England, into a rented home called Ravensbrook with Cora, her companion Mrs. Ruedy, Greek refugees—twins—and a puppy. He combined his war experiences to write another short story, "Death and the Child."

At Ravensbrook, Crane settled into domestic life, entertaining friends, including H.G. Wells, Ford Madox Ford, and Joseph Conrad. Conrad and Crane became especially close friends, and Conrad left a reminiscence of the friendship that is particularly telling and memorable, beginning with an affectionate physical description:

> Most of the true Stephen Crane was in his eyes, most of his strength at any rate, though it was apparent also in his other features, as, for instance, in the structure of his forehead, the deep solid arches under the fair eyebrows. . . . Contempt and indignation never broke the surface of his moderation, simply because he had no surface. He was all through of the same material, incapable of affectation of any kind, of any pitiful failure of generosity for the sake of personal advantage, or even from sheer exasperation which must find its relief.

Toward the middle of the essay, Conrad speaks of one particular visit by Crane, revealing the almost mystical affinity the two shared:

> He came on a flying visit to Pent Farm where we were living then. I noticed that he looked harassed. I, too, was feeling for the moment as if things were getting too much for me. He lay

on the couch and I sat on a chair opposite. After a longish silence, in which we both could have felt how uncertain was the
issue of life envisaged as a deadly adventure in which we were
both engaged like two men trying to keep afloat in a small
boat, I said suddenly across the width of the mantel-piece:

"None of them knew the colour of the sky." [Conrad quotes
the memorable first line from "The Open Boat."]

He raised himself sharply. The words had struck him as
familiar, though I believe he failed to place them at first.
"Don't you know that quotation?" I asked. . . . The startled expression passed off his face. "Oh, yes," he said quietly, and lay
down again. Truth to say, it was a time when neither he nor
I had leisure to look up idly at the sky.

Finally, Conrad gives an irresistible portrait of life at Crane's
home and also of his relationship with Conrad's infant son,
Borys:

> The best yet are the Crane dogs, a very important part of the
> establishment and quite conscious of it, belonging apparently
> to some order of outlandish poodles, amazingly sedate, and
> yet the most restless animals I have ever met. They pervaded,
> populated, and filled the whole house. Whichever way one
> looked at any time—down the passage up the stairs, into the
> drawing-room—there was always a dog in sight. Had I been
> asked on the first day how many there were, I would have
> guessed about thirty. As a matter of fact there were only three,
> but I think they never sat down, except in Crane's study,
> where they had their entree at all hours.

> He loved children; but his friendship with our child was of
> the kind that put our mutual sentiment, by comparison,
> somewhere within the Arctic region. . . . I have never detected
> Crane stretched full length on his elbows on a grass plot, in
> order to gaze at me; on the other hand, this was his usual at-
> titude of communion with the small child—with him who
> was called *the Boy*. . . .

> Glancing out of the low window of my room I would see
> them, very still, staring at each other with a solemn under-
> standing that needed no words, or perhaps was beyond words
> altogether. I could not object on any ground to their profound
> intimacy, but I do not see why Crane should have developed
> such an unreasonable suspicion as to my paternal efficiency.
> He seemed to be everlastingly taking the boy's part. I could
> not see that the baby was being oppressed, hectored over, or
> in any way deprived of its rights, or ever wounded in its feel-
> ings by me; but Crane seemed always to nurse some vague
> unexpressed grievance as to my conduct. I was inconsiderate.
> For instance—why could I not get a dog for the boy? One day
> he made quite a scene about it. He seemed to imply I should
> drop everything and go look for a dog. I sat under the storm
> and said nothing. At last he cried, "Hang it all, a boy ought to

have a dog." It was an appeal to first principles, but for an answer I pointed at the window and said: "Behold the boy.". . . He was sitting on a rug spread on the grass, with his little red stocking-cap very much over one eye (a fact of which he seemed unaware), and propped round with many pillows on account of his propensity to roll over on his side helplessly. My answer was irresistible. This is one of the few occasions on which I heard Stephen Crane laugh outright. He dropped his preaching on the dog theme and went out to the boy while I went on with my work. But he was strangely incorrigible. When he came back after an hour or so, his first words were, "Joseph, I will teach your boy to ride." I closed with the offer at once—but it was not to be. He was not given the time.

Besides his entertaining at Ravensbrook, Crane wrote— furiously—to earn money. Both Cora and Crane liked to entertain and live lavishly, and, in order to maintain the lifestyle, Crane wrote, though he was never able to keep out of debt. His most well known works from this period are "The Monster," "The Bride Comes to Yellow Sky," "Five White Mice," and "The Blue Hotel."

On February 15, 1897, the USS *Maine* was blown up in Havana harbor. The U.S. government became convinced that Spain was responsible and began to speak of joining the war on the side of Cuba. Crane, as usual, desperately wanted to participate, and went to a navy recruitment office in New York to join the navy. Although he was rejected (some scholars speculate that navy examiners told him he had tuberculosis), he decided to go anyway as a war correspondent for the *World.* Crane spent his time in the Spanish-American War following the U.S. Marines as they fought at Daiquiri, Las Guasimas, El Caney, and San Juan Hill before the surrender of Santiago on July 14. The rigorous physical regimen was too much for him, however, and he became deathly ill not only from the tuberculosis, but also with a severe case of malaria.

Ordered to evacuate to Virginia, he recuperated in a hospital. When he made it to the *World* office in July, he found that he had been fired for, among other things, being scooped on covering important battles and helping a wounded correspondent by writing his story for him and sending it to a competing newspaper.

Discouraged, he went to Puerto Rico and then back to Havana, wired stories from Havana for the New York *Journal* through most of September, and then basically disappeared. Although his mysterious withdrawal into private life has never been fully explained, Crane did return to writing—prodigiously.

He then moved to New York briefly, and then back to England to a ruined manor house that Cora had rented called Brede Place. Some scholars say that Brede Place in Sussex was a death trap for someone with tuberculosis: It was huge, unheated, without electricity, and located in the heart of damp and chilly English countryside. Nevertheless, Crane kept up a prodigious output of work, including poems and many short stories, including *Whilomville Stories* and "The Upturned Face." All the while, his tuberculosis worsened and he began to question friends about potential health resorts.

His poor health did little to deter his appetite for entertaining, however, and the Cranes planned a huge party for the end of December 1899. Each of the guests was to write a word or line for a play Crane called *The Ghost.* Crane hoped that the guest list, which included Henry James, Joseph Conrad, H.G. Wells, and others, would produce something amusing.

The party began on December 27 and the play was performed the next day. On December 29, after staying up until 3:00 A.M. with his guests, Crane suffered a massive hemorrhage. For almost four months, Crane was a virtual invalid, never leaving his house. Then, on March 31, he hemorrhaged twice more and Cora moved him to Bedenweiler in the Black Forest in a vain attempt at recovery. On June 5, 1900, at the age of twenty-nine, the author of *The Red Badge of Courage* died.

CHAPTER 1

Themes and Style in the Work of Stephen Crane

READINGS ON STEPHEN CRANE

Stephen Crane Ranks Among the Great Writers

H.G. Wells

English novelist H.G. Wells (1866–1946) is a well-known writer of science fiction, including *The Time Machine* and *The War of the Worlds*, as well as a history of the Western world, *Outline of History*. In the following article, Wells gives a brief overview of many of Crane's works, concluding that, though he died early and his work is flawed, Crane deserves to be counted among the great writers.

The untimely death at thirty [twenty-eight] of Stephen Crane robs English literature of an interesting and significant figure, and the little world of those who write, of a stout friend and a pleasant comrade. For a year and more he had been ailing. The bitter hardships of his Cuban expedition had set its mark upon mind and body alike, and the slow darkling of the shadow upon him must have been evident to all who were not blinded by their confidence in what he was yet to do. Altogether, I knew Crane for less than a year, and I saw him for the last time hardly more than seven weeks ago. He was then in a hotel at Dover, lying still and comfortably wrapped about, before an open window and the calm and spacious sea. If you would figure him as I saw him, you must think of him as a face of a type very typically American, long and spare, with very straight hair and straight features and long, quiet hands and hollow eyes, moving slowly, smiling and speaking slowly, with that deliberate New Jersey manner he had, and lapsing from speech again into a quiet contemplation of his ancient enemy. For it was the sea that had taken his strength, the same sea that now shone, level waters beyond level waters, with here and there a minute, shining ship, warm and tranquil beneath the tranquil evening

Reprinted from H.G. Wells, "Stephen Crane: From an English Standpoint," *North American Review*, August 1900.

sky. Yet I felt scarcely a suspicion then that this was a last meeting. One might have seen it all, perhaps. He was thin and gaunt and wasted, too weak for more than a remembered jest and a greeting and good wishes. It did not seem to me in any way credible that he would reach his refuge in the Black Forest only to die at the journey's end. It will be a long time yet before I can fully realize that he is no longer a contemporary of mine; that the last I saw of him was, indeed, final and complete.

Though my personal acquaintance with Crane was so soon truncated, I have followed his work for all the four years it has been known in England. I have always been proud, and now I am glad, that, however obscurely, I also was in the first chorus of welcome that met his coming. It is, perhaps, no great distinction for me; he was abundantly praised; but, at least, I was early and willing to praise him when I was wont to be youthfully jealous of my praises. His success in England began with "The Red Badge of Courage," which did, indeed, more completely than any other book has done for many years, taken the reading public by storm. Its freshness of method, its vigor of imagination, its force of color and its essential freedom from many traditions that dominate this side of the Atlantic, came—in spite of the previous shock of Mr. Kipling—with a positive effect of impact. It was a new thing, in a new school. When one looked for sources, one thought at once of Tolstoi; but, though it was clear that Tolstoi had exerted a powerful influence upon the conception, if not the actual writing, of the book, there still remained something entirely original and novel. To a certain extent, of course, that was the new man as an individual; but, to at least an equal extent, it was the new man as a typical young American, free at last, as no generation of Americans have been free before, of any regard for English criticism, comment or tradition, and applying to literary work the conception and theories of the cosmopolitan studio with a quite American directness and vigor. For the great influence of the studio on Crane cannot be ignored; in the persistent selection of the essential elements of an impression, in the ruthless exclusion of mere information, in the direct vigor with which the selected points are made, there is Whistler even more than there is Tolstoi in "The Red Badge of Courage." And witness this, taken almost haphazard:

> At nightfall the column broke into regimental pieces, and the fragments went into the fields to camp. Tents sprang up like strange plants. Camp fires, like red, peculiar blossoms, dotted the night. . . . From this little distance the many fires, with the black forms of men passing to and fro before the crimson rays, made weird and satanic effects.

And here again; consider the daring departure from all academic requirements, in this void countenance:

> A warm and strong hand clasped the youth's languid fingers for an instant, and then he heard a cheerful and audacious whistling as the man strode away. As he who had so be-friended him was thus passing out of his life, it suddenly oc-curred to the youth that he had not once seen his face.

I do not propose to add anything here to the mass of criticism upon this remarkable book. Like everything else which has been abundantly praised, it has occasionally been praised "all wrong;" and I suppose that it must have been said hundreds of times that this book is a subjective study of the typical soldier in war. But Mr. George Wyndham, himself a soldier of experience, has pointed out . . . the hero of the "Red Badge" is, and is intended to be, altogether a more sensitive and imaginative person than the ordinary man. He is the idealist, the dreamer of boastful things brought suddenly to the test of danger and swift occasions and the presence of death. To this theme Crane returned several times, and particularly in a story called "Death and the Child" that was written after the Greek war. That story is considered by very many of Crane's admirers as absolutely his best. I have carefully re-read it in deference to opinions I am bound to respect, but I still find it inferior to the earlier work. The generalized application is, to my taste, a little too evidently underlined; there is just that touch of insistence that prevails so painfully at times in Victor Hugo's work, as of a writer not sure of his reader, not happy in his reader and seeking to drive his implication (of which also he is not quite sure) home. The child is not a natural child; there is no happy touch to make it personally alive; it is THE CHILD, something unfalteringly big; a large, pink, generalized thing, I cannot help but see it, after the fashion of a Vatican cherub. The fugitive runs panting to where, all innocent of the battle about it, it plays; and he falls down breathless to be asked, "Are you a man?" One sees the intention clearly enough; but in the later story it seems to me there is a new ingredient that is absent from the earlier stories, an ingredient imposed on Crane's natural genius from without—a concession to the demands of a criticism it had been wiser, if less modest, in him to disregard—criticism that missed this quality of generalization and demanded it, even though it had to be artificially and deliberately introduced.

COMPULSION OF SYMPATHY

Following hard upon the appearance of "The Red Badge of Courage" in England came reprints of two books, "Maggie" and "George's Mother," that had already appeared in America six years earlier. Their reception gave Crane his first taste of the peculiarities of the new public he had come upon. These stories seem to me in no way inferior to the "Red Badge;" and at times there are passages, the lament of Maggie's mother at the end of "Maggie," for example, that it would be hard to beat by any passage from the later book. But on all hands came discouragement or tepid praise. The fact of it is, there had been almost an orgie of praise—for England, that is; and ideas and adjectives and phrases were exhausted. To write further long reviews on works displaying the same qualities as had been already amply discussed in the notices of the "Red Badge" would be difficult and laborious; while to admit an equal excellence and deny an equal prominence would be absurd. But to treat these stories as early work, to find them immature, dismiss them and proceed to fresher topics, was obvious and convenient. So it was, I uncharitably imagine, that these two tales have been overshadowed and are still comparatively unknown. Yet, they are absolutely essential to a just understanding of Crane. In these stories, and in these alone, he achieved tenderness and a compulsion of sympathy for other than vehement emotions, qualities that the readers of "The Third Violet" and "On Active Service," his later love stories, might well imagine beyond his reach.

And upon the appearance of these books in England came what, in my present mood, I cannot but consider as the great blunder and misfortune of Crane's life. It is a trait of the public we writers serve, that to please it is to run the gravest risk of never writing again. Through a hundred channels and with a hundred varieties of seduction and compulsion, the public seeks to induce its favorite to do something else—to act, to lecture, to travel, to jump down volcanoes or perform in music halls, to do anything, rather than to possess his soul in peace and to pursue the work he was meant to do. Indeed, this modern public is as violently experimental with its writers as a little child with a kitten. It is animated, above all things, by an insatiable desire to plunge its victim into novel surroundings, and watch how he feels. And since Crane had demonstrated, beyond all cavil, that he could sit at home and, with nothing but his wonderful brain and his wonderful induction from recorded things, build up the truest and most convincing picture of war; since he was a fastidious and careful worker, intensely subjective in his mental habit; since he was a man of fragile physique and of that unreasonable courage that will wreck the strongest physique; and since, moreover, he was habitually a bad traveller, losing trains and luggage and missing connections even in the orderly circumstances of peace, it was clearly the most reasonable thing in the world to propose, it was received with the applause of two hemispheres as a most right and proper thing, that he should go as a war correspondent, first to Greece and then to Cuba. Thereby, and for nothing but disappointment and bitterness, he utterly wrecked his health. He came into comparison with men as entirely his masters in this work as he was the master of all men in his own; and I read even in the most punctual of his obituary notices the admission of his journalistic failure. I have read, too, that he brought back nothing from these expeditions. But, indeed, even not counting his death, he brought back much. On his way home from Cuba [actually on his way to Cuba from Florida] he was wrecked, and he wrote the story ["The Open Boat"] of the nights and days that followed the sinking of the ship with a simplicity and vigor that even he cannot rival elsewhere.

"THE OPEN BOAT"

"The Open Boat" is to my mind, beyond all question, the crown of all his work. It has all the stark power of the earlier stories, with a new element of restraint; the color is as full and strong as ever, fuller and stronger, indeed; but those chromatic splashes that at times deafen and confuse in "The Red Badge," those images that astonish rather than enlighten, are disciplined and controlled. "That and 'Flanagan'," he told me, with a philosophical laugh, "was all I got out of Cuba." I cannot say whether they were worth the price, but I am convinced that these two things are as immortal as any work of any living man. And the way "The Open Boat" begins, no stress, plain—even a little gray and flattish. . . .

From that beginning, the story mounts and mounts over the waves, wave frothing after wave, each wave a threat, and the men toil and toil and toil again; by insensible degrees the day lights the waves to green and olive, and the foam grows dazzling. Then as the long day draws out, they come toward the land.

A Tangible Writer

Crane is never obscure. The first of the imagists, he never becomes jagged in his manner, nor sacrifices movement to the elaboration of striking detail. To call him a journalist of genius helps to define him, but there still remains the problem of his haunting charm. That charm springs, in large measure, from his free, courageous mind. Lucidity like his is poetry. Even when he is journalistically crude and incorrect, as he often is, he reveals an intelligence working acutely upon its observations. He has therefore the smallest possible burden of nonsense to carry with him. He does not worry himself with insoluble mysteries, such as the duties of the cosmic whole to the finite individual.

> A man said to the universe:
> "Sir, I exist!"
> "However," replied the universe,
> "The fact had not created in me
> A sense of obligation."

Thus jauntily Crane can dismiss the larger metaphysics. He works within a tangible area. And when his intelligence has brought him close to his material he feels for it the desire of a lover. That he sees life under the light of irony does not diminish his passion but increases it. Are these characters, these situations, these comic or tragic consequences, after all, only the brief concerns of fate? Doubtless. But they have importance for the ephemeral creatures who are involved in them. And they have pattern and color for the unduped yet affectionate spectator.

Carl Van Doren, "Stephen Crane," *American Mercury*, vol. 1, January 1924.

"The Open Boat" gives its title to a volume containing, in addition to that and "Flanagan," certain short pieces. One of these others, at least, is also to my mind a perfect thing, "The Wise Men." It tells of the race between two bar-tenders in the city of Mexico, and I cannot imagine how it could possibly have been better told. And in this volume, too, is that other masterpiece—the one I deny—"Death and the Child."

Now I do not know how Crane took the reception of this book, for he was not the man to babble of his wrongs; but I cannot conceive how it could have been anything but a grave disappointment to him. To use the silly phrase of the literary shopman, "the vogue of the short story" was already over; rubbish, pure rubbish, provided only it was lengthy, had resumed its former precedence again in the reviews, in the publishers' advertisements and on the library and book-sellers' counters. The book was taken as a trivial by-product, its author was exhorted to abandon this production of "brilliant fragments"—anything less than fifty thousand words is a fragment to the writer of literary columns—and to make that "sustained effort," that architectural undertaking, that alone impresses the commercial mind. Of course, the man who can call "The Open Boat" a brilliant fragment would reproach Rodin for not completing the edifice his brilliant fragments of statuary are presumably intended to adorn, and would sigh, with the late Mr. Ruskin for the day when Mr. Whistler would "finish" his pictures. Moreover, he was strongly advised—just as they have advised Mr. Kipling—to embark upon a novel. And from other quarters, where a finer wisdom might have been displayed, he learned that the things he had written were not "short stories" at all; they were "sketches" perhaps, "anecdotes"—just as they call Mr. Kipling's short stories "anecdotes;" and it was insinuated that for him also the true, the ineffable "short story" was beyond his reach. I think it is indisputable that the quality of this reception, which a more self-satisfied or less sensitive man than Crane might have ignored, did react very unfavorably upon his work. They put him out of conceit with these brief intense efforts in which his peculiar strength was displayed.

It was probably such influence that led him to write "The Third Violet." I do not know certainly, but I imagine, that the book was to be a demonstration, and it is not a successful demonstration, that Crane could write a charming love story. It is the very simple affair of an art student and a summer boarder, with the more superficial incidents of their petty encounters set forth in a forcible, objective manner that is curiously hard and unsympathetic. The characters act, and on reflection one admits they act, *true*, but the play of their emotions goes on behind the curtain of the style, and all the enrichments of imaginative appeal that make love beautiful are omitted. Yet, though the story as a whole fails to satisfy, there are many isolated portions of altogether happy effectiveness, a certain ride behind an ox cart, for example. Much more surely is "On Active Service" an effort, and in places a painful effort, to fit his peculiar gift to the uncongenial conditions of popular acceptance. It is the least capable and least satisfactory of all Crane's work.

WAR POETRY

While these later books were appearing, and right up to his last fatal illness, Crane continued to produce fresh war pictures that show little or no falling off in vigor of imagination and handling; and, in addition, he was experimenting with verse. In that little stone-blue volume, "War is Kind," and in the earlier "Black Riders," the reader will find a series of acute and vivid impressions and many of the finer qualities of Crane's descriptive prose, but he will not find any novel delights of melody or cadence or any fresh aspects of Crane's personality. There remain some children's stories [*Whilomville Stories*] to be published and an unfinished romance [*The O'Ruddy*]. With that the tale of his published work ends, and the career of one of the most brilliant, most significant and most distinctively American of all English writers comes to its unanticipated *finis*.

It would be absurd, here and now, to attempt to apportion any relativity of importance to Crane, to say that he was greater than A. or less important than B. That class-list business is, indeed, best left forever to the newspaper plebiscite and the library statistician; among artists, whose sole, just claim to recognition and whose sole title to immortality must necessarily be the possession of unique qualities, that is to say, of unclassifiable factors, these gradations are absurd. Suffice it that, even before his death, Crane's right to be counted in the hierarchy of those who have made a permanent addition to the great and growing fabric of English letters was not only assured, but conceded. To define his position in time, however, and in relation to periods and modes of writing will be a more reasonable undertaking; and it seems to me that, when at last the true proportions can be seen, Crane will be found to occupy a position singularly cardinal. He was a New Englander of Puritan lineage, and the son of a long tradition of literature. There had been many Cranes who wrote before him. He has shown me a shelf of books, for the most part the pious and theological works of various antecedent Stephen Cranes. He had been at some pains to gather together these alien products of his kin. For the most part they seemed little, insignificant books, and one opened them to read the beaten *clichés*, the battered outworn phrases, of a movement that has ebbed. Their very size and binding suggested a dying impulse, that very same impulse that in its prime had carried the magnificence of Milton's imagery and the pomp and splendors of Milton's prose. In Crane that impulse was altogether dead. He began stark—I find all through this brief notice I have been repeating that in a dozen disguises, "freedom from tradition," "absolute directness" and the like—as though he came into the world of letters without ever a predecessor. In style, in method and in all that is distinctively *not* found in his books, he is sharply defined, the expression in literary art of certain enormous repudiations. Was ever a man before who wrote of battles so abundantly as he has done, and never had a word, never a word from first to last, of the purpose and justification of the war? And of the God of Battles, no more than the battered name; "Hully Gee!"—the lingering trace of the Deity! And of the sensuousness and tenderness of love, so much as one can find in "The Third Violet!" Any richness of allusion, any melody or balance of phrase, the half quotation that refracts and softens and enriches the statement, the momentary digression that opens like a window upon beautiful or distant things, are not merely absent, but obviously and sedulously avoided. It is as if the racial thought and tradition had been razed from his mind and its site ploughed and salted. He is more than himself in this; he is the first expression of the opening mind of a new period, or, at least, the early emphatic phase of a new initiative—beginning, as a growing mind must needs begin, with the record of impressions, a record of a vigor and intensity beyond all precedent.

Crane's Writing Is Disappointing

Alfred Kazin

Alfred Kazin is a well-known literary critic and writer praised for his works *On Native Grounds* and the autobiographical *New York Jew*. In the following article, Kazin analyzes Crane's work, finding it "curiously thin, and, in one sense, even corrupt." Kazin argues that Crane's writing, though redeemable, is deeply flawed.

Out of this welter of enthusiasms that gave so many different clues to the future, there now emerged at the end of the century the one creative artist who sounded the possibilities open to his generation, though he fulfilled so few of them himself. In his day Stephen Crane stood as . . . the fever-ridden, rigidly intense type of genius that dies young, unhappy, and the prey of lady biographers. Everything that he wrote in his twenty-nine years seemed without precedent. . . . But no conventional background or stimulus explains Crane's disposition to naturalism; neither the depression of the nineties, which never troubled him, nor the classic texts of European naturalism, by which he was generally bored. He was a naturalist by birth, so to speak; but there is nothing in the placid Jersey parsonage of the Reverend Jonathan Crane that explains the grim finality of mind, in its way an astounding capacity for tragedy, that devoured his fourteenth child. Sentimental critics have charged that Crane had a secret disaffection born out of his father's martyrdom in the service of Methodism and its apparent futility in the face of world events, but the surest thing one can say about Crane is that he cared not a jot which way the world went. No one was ever less the reforming mind; revolutions were something foreigners attempted that Hearst would pay good money to report. He accepted the world always, hating it always, plotting his way through it alone with a contempt that was close to pain.

Thomas Beer, who understood him best, hit at the secret of Crane's career when he wrote of a ruthless literary courage possible only to those who are afraid. Life tossed him up and down like a cork. To his last days he was tormented by disease and insecurity, greedy friends and witnesses of his genius who thought him a strangely convivial freak, stupid editors and pristine reviewers, the doltish open mouth of the public, pointing, giggling, and retailing stories. Crane never had a juvenile period, a time of test and error, of sentimental amplitude and human indirection. The hard, fixed boundaries which hold his books were iron clamps which were set early. All through that miserably unhappy life, even in the first days of glory when *The Red Badge of Courage* fell out of the heavens, he was the stricken boy Conrad saw at the end in Brede Place in England, sitting in a baronial pile eating his heart out in hack work, devoured by sycophants, always in some portentous torment, with the suffering eyes and the absurd mustache that fell over his face like the mask of old age.

The world was a ship, he wrote in one of his poems, that God had fashioned and let slip.

> God fashioned the ship of the world carefully.
> With the infinite skill of an All-Master
> Made He the hull and the sails,
> Held He the rudder
> Ready for adjustment.
> Erect stood He, scanning his work proudly.
> Then—at fateful time—a wrong called,
> And God turned, heeding.
> Lo, the ship, at this opportunity, slipped slyly,
>   · · · · · · · ·
> Making quaint progress,
> Turning as with serious purpose
> Before stupid winds.
> And there were many in the sky
> Who laughed at this thing.

And no more than God could he hope to reclaim it. "I cannot be shown," he said once, "that God bends on us any definable stare, like a sergeant at muster, and his laughter would be bully to hear out in nothingness." He would not appeal against wrong, and he thought it monstrous to complain. Essentially uneducated, his resources lay in his physical senses, which he exploited with an intensity disproportionate to his strength and yet unequal to the fervor of his spirit. He read very little, and nothing surprised him more than when people who read his work condescendingly discovered his debt to Zola or to Tolstoy. *War and Peace*, which he knew, stimulated him to the boyish cockiness that flared at rare instances and was one of his more charming traits. "Tolstoy could have done the whole business in one-third of the time and made it just as wonderful," he laughed. "It goes on and on like Texas." He thought of writing a book entitled *Peace and War*, which would do "the job" better and be an answer to Tolstoy. It was perhaps because he had read so little, as Willa Cather suggested, that he felt no responsibility to be accurate or painstaking in his transcription of common events. Like every sensuous artist, he was a magnificent guesser, and nothing proved how deeply he had imagined the psychology of battle in *The Red Badge of Courage* than his experience as correspondent in the Greco-Turkish War. "*The Red Badge* is all right," he said when he came out of it.

Yet the stark greatness of the novel did grow in part out of his instinctively intimate knowledge of American manners and character. As Carl Van Doren observed, the verisimilitude of the book testified to Crane's knowledge of the popular memory and authentic legends of the war. One side of him was the local village boy who never quite lost his feeling for the small talk and the casual pleasures of the American town, and it showed not only in the campfire talk of the men in *The Red Badge*, but in the charming little-boy stories in *Whilomville Stories* and the extraordinary transcriptions of Negro speech in *The Monster*. What kept Crane alive, in one sense, was just that feeling; without it his despair might have seemed intolerable and, for an artist of his sensibility, incommunicable. He baited the universe but never those village citizens who are as benign in his work as small-town fathers in the *Saturday Evening Post*. They were his one medium of fraternity, and his strong, quiet affection for them testifies to the unconscious strength of his personal citizenship.

A TALE OF EVERYMAN

In this sense even the most astonishing effects in *The Red Badge of Courage* reflect Crane's background, for its soldier-hero might have been any American boy suddenly removed from the farm to fight in a war of whose issues he knew little and in which his predominating emotion was one of consummate perplexity and boredom. As a novelist of war Crane anticipated the war studies of the future. . . . Crane's hero is Everyman, the symbol made flesh upon which war plays its havoc; and it is the deliberation of that intention which explains why the novel is so extraordinarily lacking, as H.L. Mencken put it, in small talk. Scene follows scene in an accelerating rhythm of excitement, the hero becomes the ubiquitous man to whom, as Wyndham Lewis once wrote of the Hemingway hero, things happen. With that cold, stricken fury that was so characteristic of Crane—all through the self-conscious deliberation of his work one can almost hear his nerves quiver—he impaled his hero on the ultimate issue, the ultimate pain and humiliation of war, where the whole universe, leering through the blindness and smoke of battle, became the incarnation of pure agony. The foreground was a series of commonplaces; the background was cosmological. Crane had driven so quickly through to the central problem that everything else seemed accessory in its effect, but he was forced to describe emotions in terms of color because the pressure behind so wholly concentrated a force drove him to seek unexpected and more plastic sources of imagery. Often he revealed himself to be a very deliberate tone-painter, as calculating and even mechanical a worker in the magnificent as Oscar Wilde or Richard Strauss. He aimed at picture qualities and he synthesized them so neatly that, like the movement of the hunters and the hunted in a tapestry of the medieval chase, they illustrated a world whose darkness was immensity. "In the Eastern sky there was a yellow patch, like a rug laid for the feet of the coming sun; and against it, black and pattern-like, loomed the gigantic figure of the colonel on a gigantic horse."

A WEARINESS OF LIFE

Yet for all its beauty, Crane's best work was curiously thin and, in one sense, even corrupt. His desperation exhausted him too quickly; his unique sense of tragedy was a monotone. No one in America had written like him before; but though his books precipitately gave the whole esthetic movement of the nineties a sudden direction and a fresher impulse, he could contribute no more than the intensity of his spirit. Half of him was a consummate workman; the other half was not a writer at all. In his ambitious stories of New York tenement life, *Maggie* and *George's Mother*, the violence seemed almost celestial, but it was only Crane's own, and verbal; both stories suffer from excessive hardness and that strangely clumsy diction that Crane never learned to polish. In a great show piece like *The Open Boat* (drawn from an almost direct report of experiences in the Caribbean in the days when he was reporting the Cuban insurrection for New York newspapers) he proved himself the first great pyrotechnician of the contemporary novel; but the few superb stories are weighed down by hack work. The man who wrote *The Blue Hotel* also wrote more trash than any other serious novelist of his time. Even in buffooneries like his unfinished last novel, *The O'Ruddy*, there is the sense of a wasted talent flowing over the silly improvisation in silent derision. He had begun by astonishing the contemporary mind into an acceptance of new forms; he ended by parodying Richard Harding Davis in *Active Service* and [Robert Louis] Stevenson in *The O'Ruddy*. Yet it was not frustration that wore him out, but his own weariness of life. His gift was a furious one, but barren; writing much, he repeated himself so joylessly that in the end he seemed to be mocking himself with the same quiet viciousness with which, even as a boy, he had mocked the universe. An old child, it was not merely by his somberness that he anticipated the misanthropy of the twentieth-century novel. Pride and a fiercely quaking splendor mark his first and last apotheosis: he was the first great tragic figure in the modern American generation.

Crane Is a Parodist

Eric Solomon

Eric Solomon is a critic and author of the book
Stephen Crane: From Parody to Realism, in which he
argues that Crane's roots as a writer lie in humorous
tales. In this section from Solomon's book, he analyzes *The Red Badge of Courage* in terms of Crane's
parody: in general, of the approach to war taken by
writers who came before him, and in particular, of
his hero, Henry Fleming. Solomon praises Crane's
ability to mock, then strip away, Fleming's idealistic
dreams of battle to get at the true courage Fleming
displays by book's end.

The Red Badge of Courage (1895) stands by itself in
nineteenth-century English and American war fiction. Indeed, it is still the masterwork in English among the abun-
dance of war novels that two world conflicts and dozens of
smaller wars have produced. Stephen Crane's novel is the
first work of any length in English fiction purely dedicated
to an artistic reproduction of war, and it has rarely been approached in craft or intensity. The novel became part of the
literary heritage of the twentieth century, and whether or
not a modern war writer consciously recalls Crane's performance in the genre, *The Red Badge of Courage* remains, in
Matthew Arnold's term, a touchstone for modern war fiction. Crane gave the war novel its classic form.

Of course, in writing about war, Crane drew on a form of
fiction that was more traditional than any of the other genres in which he worked. In the nineteenth century, war novels of one kind or another appeared from such authors of
historical romances as Sir Walter Scott, James Fenimore
Cooper, and William Gilmore Simms, whose books re-
sounded with battle scenes, thrilling chases, valiant heroes.
All these novelists had in common a predilection for abstract
terminology and a custom of interspersing the combat
scenes among Gothic or other domestic plot episodes. Other

writers like the Englishman George Gleig or the Irishman Charles Lever wrote of battle as a rollicking adventure. William Makepeace Thackeray dealt with war only obliquely while avoiding combat scenes—but did savagely mock the concept of military heroism—and later in the century Rudyard Kipling, in a rather embarrassed manner, glorified the joys and brutalities of military life.

By the time American novelists began writing about the Civil War, a European tradition of irony and realism, and a motif of the development, through war, from innocence to maturity, had been established through the war fiction of De Vigny, Stendhal, Zola, and Tolstoy. For the most part, however, American war fiction was hardly realistic. . . . The Civil War was usually a background for a stirring love story often complicated by the Northern versus Southern brother theme. One of Charles King's novels describes its hero as "an ardent patriot, an enthusiastic soldier, a born cavalryman." These three phrases might delineate the viewpoint of the great mass of Civil War potboilers, romances, and dime novels: the patriotic element provided the controlling theme, battle was spirited and chivalric, and the hero was a born soldier who needed to undergo no tempering process through war. . . . Throughout the nineteenth century war was, in popular fiction—with some exceptions—not a serious metaphor for life. If there was a norm for war fiction, it was the flashing-sword and magnolia-blossom novels of [John Ester] Cooke and his followers. Perhaps the plot of an anonymous tale that appeared in the New York *Daily Tribune* on July 19, 1891, will exemplify the traditions against which Stephen Crane was reacting when he conceived his war novel. "Thompson of Ours" is the jolly account of a noble young officer who saves his comrades by riding like the wind to bring aid, though concealing a serious wound. Among his many heroics, this generous act of hiding his wound earns the lovable daredevil the Victoria Cross. Crane, by writing of a hero who reverses the romantic ideal and pretends to have a wound where he actually received none, parodied the heroic and set a pattern of antiheroics. . . .

CRANE'S UNIQUE CONTRIBUTIONS

The contribution of Crane to the genre of war fiction was twofold. First, he defined in his novel the form that deals with war and its effect upon the sensitive individual who is inextricably involved; he uses war as a fictional test of mind and spirit in a situation of great tension. Also he constructed a book that still stands as the technical masterpiece in the field.

Crane accomplishes in the longer form of the novel what [Ambrose] Bierce attained in the short story. *The Red Badge of Courage* creates a single world, a unique atmosphere where war is the background and the foreground. . . . Crane works within a tightly restricted area. He writes a kind of grammar in which war is the subject, the verb, and the object of every sentence. Like the painters of the Italian Renaissance who conceived the *tondo*, a form that forced the artist to choose and manipulate his subject matter to fit a small circular canvas, Crane chose to restrict his novel to war and its impact upon his hero. There is no mention of the causes or motives of the war or of any battle; Crane's war is universal, extricated from any specific historical situation. We may gain an impression of how a literary artist makes a *tondo* of war by an analysis of the structure of *The Red Badge of Courage.* For Crane approached the subject of war as an artist, picking his materials for their fictional value. He was not reliving an experience but creating one. As for the conception of the novel, "It was an effort born of pain," states the author. *The Red Badge of Courage* employs previous assumptions about heroic soldiers that informed almost all popular Civil War fiction before the rise of realism in the 1890's in order to reject them. He parodies, then, an approach to war rather than a body of war fiction; thus his book survives long after the immediate occasion for its germination is forgotten, survives as creative art, not as critical comment. Crane synthesizes parody with reality, integrates parodic, realistic, and, of course, imaginative visions into a unity. He subtly distorts the traditions rather than creating a new inverted form; his method is allusive satire rather than direct travesty.

OBLIQUE PARODY

Unlike many of his other novels where Crane starts with direct burlesque of a traditional form, *The Red Badge of Courage* uses parody obliquely. By making his hero anonymous for much of the novel and by investing him with cowardly instincts, Crane does away with the traditional cliché of war fiction, the bravery of the hero. As we have noticed, earlier nineteenth-century war fiction, with the exception of

Bierce's short pieces, leaned on either a love story or a historical framework. Crane glances at this custom by having Henry immediately imagine a briefly seen dark-haired girl to be in love with his heroic person. This tiny scene, early in the novel, is Crane's deliberately brief bow to the usual materials of war fiction, for the girl is never spoken of again. Only war can define Crane's protagonist: "He finally concluded that the only way to prove himself was to go into the blaze."

From start to finish Crane's war novel is shot through with mockery of the common views of war that marked the bulk of the century's war fiction. Like Henry Fleming himself, Crane commits many "crimes against the gods of tradition." Most obviously, his hero is no familiar hero: he is a coward, a deserter, a liar. And, like Cervantes' mocked knight, Henry has rooted his warlike dreams in reading about "vague and bloody conflicts that had thrilled him with their sweep and fire . . . a Greeklike struggle . . . distinctly Homeric. . . . He had read of marches, sieges, conflicts. . . . His busy mind had drawn for him large pictures extravagant in color, lurid with breathless deeds."

Crane parodies war fiction in three ways: through direct depiction of the reversal of Henry's romantic stereotypes; through the indirect characterization of Henry as a fallible, egocentric antihero; and, as always in Crane's best fiction, through the sense of reality—which by its denial of romantic illusions convinced many contemporary reviewers that the author must have been himself a war veteran. The three approaches are not distinct. They reflect back on each other and often work together. For example, when Henry overhears a general, he expects a Napoleonic phrase, but the reality refers to a box of cigars. Later he expects another general to request information from the private—for that is the way it is in dime novels. And the lesson that fictional generalizations are invalid is one element of the youth's wartime education. Those men are absurd who "supposed that they were cutting the letters of their names deep into the everlasting tablets of brass." As we shall see, Henry's dreams of sublime heroism are slow to die; halfway through the novel he sees himself as a hero out of Scott or Cooke, "a blue desperate figure leading lurid charges with one knee forward and a broken blade high . . . getting calmly killed on a high place before the eyes of all." The fact that his dreams come true in part, that he does stand out heroically in the regiment's final charge, keeps the novel from any rigid, black and white contrast between dream and reality. When Henry earns his red badge, it is in an episode that travesties heroic action. But Crane's artistic and moral vision allows him to move through travesty and mock heroics to reality and genuine courage. Yet the clichés of war fiction—the past flashing before the eyes of a dying man, the return to the regiment, the educational process of the baptism of fire—are alternately mocked and used in *The Red Badge of Courage*, while the realities of combat blast literary preconceptions, the "vague feminine formula for beloved ones doing brave deeds on the field of battle without risk of life." Although Crane clearly admires Henry's ultimate combat heroism, the parodic insight protects the author from hero worship. For all his eventual success as a warrior, Henry rejects the romantic tradition. He cannot (because of his bodily aches) "persist in flying high with the wings of war; they rendered it almost impossible for him to see himself in a heroic light."

Perhaps *The Red Badge of Courage* should be termed an impressionistic-naturalistic novel. Certainly Crane uses both manners throughout. The combining of a vivid, swift montage of combat impressions with a harsh, overwhelming naturalistic view of the individuals trapped in the war machine is Crane's method of fitting the combat world into fiction. . . .

The form of *The Red Badge of Courage* represents Crane's fundamental parodic strategy. While many readers have noted the double movement of the plot, few have accepted the second half of the novel as other than repetition or a sellout to expected standards of heroism. Yet his war novel is not broken-backed. The first half focuses in a parodic manner on Henry Fleming, the antihero, isolated in his romantic literary fancies of what war should be. The second half portrays in a realistic mode the experiences of the larger body of men who muddle through. Henry is as egocentric and emotional in his bravery as in his cowardice, but Crane shows the young soldier's later action in the context of the regiment's dogged behavior. Thus the rhythm of the novel's two parts reflects the author's basic approach to fiction: the movement from parody to realism. And Henry's later heroism is not inconsistent with the first part's parodic mode; reality is not only the reverse of romance but in some ways a verification of the truths that lie behind the idealized conventions.

Crane's Fiction Depicts the Civil War in Everyday Life

Ralph Ellison

Ralph Ellison was trained as a musician at Tuskegee Institute, where he met black writer Richard Wright and became interested in writing. He won a National Book Award for his first and most well known novel, *Invisible Man.* In the following article, Ellison heralds Crane for transforming and reinterpreting events in America's history, such as the Civil War, and showing their universal application in everyday American life.

Of all our nineteenth-century masters of fiction—Hawthorne, Melville, Henry James, Mark Twain and Stephen Crane—it was Crane, the youngest, arrived most distantly from the Civil War in point of time, who was the most war-haunted. Born in Newark, New Jersey, six years after the firing ceased, Crane was the youngest of fourteen offspring of parents whose marriage marked the union of two lines of hard-preaching, fundamentalist Methodist ministers. The time and place of his birth and his parents' concern with conduct, morality and eloquence were, when joined with his self-dedication to precise feeling and writing, perhaps as portentous and as difficult a gift to bear as any seer's obligation to peer through walls and into the secret places of the heart, or around windy corners and into the enigmatic future. Indeed, such words as "clairvoyant," "occult" and "uncanny" have been used to describe his style, and while these tell us little, there was nonetheless an inescapable aura of the marvelous about Stephen Crane. For although there is no record of his eyes having been covered at birth with that caul which is said to grant one second sight, he revealed a unique vision of the human condition and an unusual talent for projecting it. His was a costly vision, won through personal suffering, hard living and harsh artistic discipline; and by the time of his death, at twenty-nine, he was recognized as one of the important innovators of American fictional prose and master of a powerful and original style.

Fortunately it was the style and not the myth which was important. Thus today, after sixty years during which there was little interest in the meaning and sources of Crane's art, the best of the work remains not only alive but capable of speaking to us with a new resonance of meaning. While recent criticism holds that the pioneer style, which leads directly to Ernest Hemingway, sprang from a dedication to the moral and aesthetic possibilities of literary form similar to that of Henry James, Crane's dedication to art was no less disciplined or deadly serious than that which characterized his preaching forefathers' concern with religion. . . .

THE EFFECTS OF CHRISTIANITY

Surely if fundamentalist Christianity could get so authoritatively into national politics (especially in the Bible Belt), so ambiguously into our system of education (as in the Scopes trial issue [pitting evolution against creationism]), into our style of crime (through prohibition's spawn of bootleggers, gangsters, jellybeans and flappers) and so powerfully into jazz—it is about time we recognized its deeper relationship to the art of our twentieth-century literature. And not simply as subject matter, but as a major source of its technique, its form and rhetoric. For while much has been made of the role of the high church in the development of modern poetry . . . Crane's example suggests that for the writer a youthful contact with the emotional intensity and harsh authority of American fundamentalism can be as important an experience as contact with those churches which possess a ritual containing elements of high art and a theology spun subtle and fine through intellectualization. Undoubtedly the Methodist Church provided Crane an early schooling in the seriousness of spiritual questions—of the individual's ultimate relationship to his fellow men, to the universe and to God—and was one source of the youthful revolt which taught him to look upon life with his own eyes. Just as important, perhaps, is the discipline which the church provided him in keeping great emotion under the control of the intellect, as during the exciting services (which the boy learned to question quite early), along with an awareness of the disparity between the individual's public testimony (a rite common to evangelical churches) and his private deeds—a matter intensified by the fact that the celebrant of this rite of public confession was his own father. In brief, Crane was concerned very early with private emotions publicly displayed as an act of purification and self-definition; an excellent beginning for a writer interested in the ordeals of the private individual struggling to define himself as against the claims of society. Crane, who might well have become a minister, turned from religion but transferred its forms to his art.

For his contemporaries much of the meaning of Crane's art was obscured by a personal myth compounded of elements ever fascinating to the American mind: his youth and his early mastery of a difficult and highly technical skill (like a precocious juvenile delinquent possessed of an uncanny knowledge not of pocket pool, craps or tap dancing, but of advanced literary technique) coupled with that highly individual way of feeling and thinking which is the basis of all significant innovation in art; his wild bohemian way of life; his maverick attitude toward respectability; his gallantry toward prostitutes no less than toward their respectable sisters; his friendship with Bowery outcasts— "What Must I Do to Be Saved?" was the title of a tract by his mother's uncle, the Methodist Bishop of Syracuse and a founder of the university there; his gambler's prodigality with fame and money; his search for wars to observe and report; and, finally, the fatality of "genius" which followed the fair, slight, gifted youth from obscurity to association with the wealthy and gifted in England (Joseph Conrad, H.G. Wells, Ford Madox Ford and Henry James were among his friends), to his death from tuberculosis, one of the period's most feared and romanticized scourges, in the far Black Forest of Germany. . . .

At the center of Crane's myth there lay, of course, the mystery of the creative talent with which a youth of twenty-one was able to write what is considered one of the world's foremost war novels when he had neither observed nor participated in combat. And, indeed, with this second book, *The Red Badge of Courage*, Crane burst upon the American public with the effect of a Civil War projectile lain dormant beneath a city square for thirty years. Two years before he had appeared with *Maggie: A Girl of the Streets*, a stripped little novel of social protest written in a strange new idiom. But although Hamlin Garland and William Dean Howells had recognized the work's importance, the reading public was prepared neither for such a close look at the devastating effect of the Bowery upon the individual's sense of life, nor for the narrow choice between the sweatshop and prostitution which Crane saw as the fate of such girls as Maggie. Besides, with its ear attuned to the languid accents of genteel fiction it was unprepared for the harsh, although offbeat, poetic realism of Crane's idiom.

In a famous inscription in which he exhorted a reader to have the "courage" to read his book to the end, Crane explained that he had tried to show that

> environment is a tremendous thing in the world, and frequently shapes lives regardless. If one proves that theory, one makes room in heaven for all sorts of souls, notably an occasional street girl, who are not confidently expected to be there by many excellent people

a statement which reveals that the young author knew the mood of his prospective audience much better than it was prepared to know him. For although Crane published *Maggie* at his own expense (significantly, under a pseudonym) and paid four men to read it conspicuously while traveling up and down Manhattan on the El, it failed.

THE RED BADGE OF COURAGE

This was for American literature a most significant failure indeed; afterward, following *Maggie*, Crane developed the strategy of understatement and the technique of impressionism which was to point the way for Hemingway and our fiction of the twenties. Crane was not to return to an explicit projection of his social criticism until "The Monster," a work written much later in his career; he turned, instead, to exploring the psychology of the individual under extreme pressure. *Maggie* . . . stands with *The Adventures of Huckleberry Finn* as one of the parents of the modern American novel; but it is *The Red Badge of Courage* which claims our attention with all the authority of a masterpiece. . . .

For all our efforts to forget it, the Civil War was the great shaping event not only of our political and economic life, but following Crane, of our twentieth-century fiction. It was the agency through which many of the conflicting elements within the old republic were brought to maximum tension, leaving us a nation fully aware of the continental character of our destiny, preparing the emergence of our predominantly industrial economy and our increasingly urban way of life, and transforming us from a nation consisting of two major regions which could pretend to a unity of values, despite their basic split over fundamental issues, to one which was now consciously divided. To put it drastically, if war, as Clausewitz insisted, is the continuation of politics by other means, it requires little imagination to see American life since the abandonment of the Reconstruction as an abrupt reversal of that formula: the continuation of the Civil War by means other than arms. In this sense the conflict has not only gone unresolved but the line between civil war and civil peace has become so blurred as to require of the sensitive man a questioning attitude toward every aspect of the nation's self-image. Stephen Crane, in his time, was such a man. . . .

In *The Red Badge* social reality is filtered through the sensibility of a young Northern soldier who is only vaguely aware of the larger issues of the war, and we note that for all the complex use of the symbolic connotations of blackness, only one Negro, a dancing teamster, appears throughout the novel. The reader is left to fill in the understated background, to re-create those matters of which the hero, Henry Fleming, is too young, too self-centered and too concerned with the more immediate problems of courage, honor and self-preservation to be aware. This leaves the real test of moral courage as much a challenge to the reader as to the hero; he must decide for himself whether or not to confront the public issues evoked by Henry's private ordeal. *The Red Badge* is a novel about a lonely individual's struggle for self-definition, written for lonely individualists, and its style, which no longer speaks in terms of the traditional American rhetoric, implies a deep skepticism as to the possibility of the old American ideals being revived by a people which had failed to live up to them after having paid so much to defend them in hardship and blood. Here in place of the conventional plot—which implies the public validity of private experiences—we find a series of vividly impressionistic episodes that convey the discontinuity of feeling and perception of one caught up in a vast impersonal action, and a concentration upon the psychology of one who seeks first to secede from society and then to live in it with honor and courage.

Indeed, for a novel supposedly about the war, *The Red Badge* is intensely concerned with invasion of the private life, a theme announced when the men encounter the body of their first dead soldier, whose shoe soles, "worn to the thinness of writing paper," strike Henry as evidence of a betrayal by fate which in death had exposed to the dead Confederate's enemies "that poverty which in life he had perhaps concealed from his friends." But war is nothing if not an invasion of privacy, and so is death (the "invulnerable" dead man forces his way between the men as they open ranks to avoid him); and society, more so. For society, even when reduced to a few companions, invades personality and demands of the individual an almost impossible consistency while guaranteeing the individual hardly anything. Or so it seems to the naïve Henry, much of whose anguish springs from the fear that his friends will discover that the wound which he received from the rifle butt of another frightened soldier is not the red badge of courage they assume but a badge of shame. Thus the Tattered Soldier's questions as to the circumstance of his injury (really questions as to his moral identity) fill Henry with fear and hostility, and he regards them as

> the assertion of a society that probed pitilessly at secrets until all is apparent. . . . His late companion's chance persistency made him feel that he could not keep his crime [of malingering] concealed in his bosom. It was sure to be brought plain by one of those arrows which cloud the air and are constantly pricking, discovering, proclaiming those things which are willed to be forever hidden. He admitted that he could not defend himself against this agency. It was not within the power of vigilance. . . .

In time Henry learns to act with honor and courage and to perceive something of what it means to be a man, but this perception depends upon the individual fates of those who make up his immediate group; upon the death of Jim Conklin, the most mature and responsible of the men, and upon the Loud Soldier's attainment of maturity and inner self-confidence. But the cost of perception is primarily personal, and for Henry it depends upon the experience of the moral discomfort which follows the crimes of malingering and assuming a phony identity, and the further crime of allowing the voice of conscience, here symbolized by the Tattered Soldier, to wander off and die. Later he acquits himself bravely and comes to feel that he has attained a quiet manhood, non-assertive but of sturdy and strong blood. He knew that he would no more quail before his guides wherever they should point. He had been to touch the great death, and found that, after all, it was but the great death. He was a man.

Obviously although Henry has been initiated into the battle of life, he has by no means finished with illusion—but that, too, is part of the human condition.

That *The Red Badge* was widely read during Crane's own time was a triumph of his art, but the real mystery lay not in his re-creation of the simpler aspects of battle: the corpses, the wounds, the sound of rifle fire, the panic and high elation of combat; the real mystery lay in the courage out of which one so young could face up to the truth which so many Americans were resisting with a noisy clamor of optimism and with frantic gestures of materialistic denial. War, the jungle and hostile Nature became Crane's underlying metaphors for the human drama and the basic situations in which the individual's capacity for moral and physical courage were put to their most meaningful testing.

"THE OPEN BOAT"

And so with "The Open Boat." In January, 1897, Crane was one of four men who spent thirty hours in a ten-foot dinghy after their ship, bound on a gun-running expedition to Cuba, developed a leak and sank. It was from this experience that Crane shaped what is considered his most perfect short story. When "The Open Boat" is compared with the report which Crane wrote for the New York *Press*, we can see that it keeps to the order of events as they actually occurred; but such is the power of Crane's shaping vision that the reader is made to *experience* the events as a complete, dynamic, symbolic action. We become one with the men in the boat, who pit their skill and courage against the raging sea, living in their hope and despair and sharing the companionship won within the capricious hand of fate. Under the shaping grace of Crane's imagination the actual event is reduced to significant form, with each wave and gust of wind, each intonation of voice and gesture of limb combining toward a single effect of meaning.

And as with most of Crane's fiction, the point at issue is the cost of moral perception, of achieving an informed sense of life, in a universe which is essentially hostile to man and in which skill and courage and loyalty are virtues which help in the struggle but by no means exempt us from the necessary plunge into the storm-sea-war of experience. For it is thus and thus only that humanity is won, and often the best are destroyed in the trial—as with Higgins, the oiler, whose skill and generosity have helped save the men from the sea but who in the end lies dead upon the shore. Through their immersion into the raging sea of life, and through Higgins's sacrificial death, the survivors are initiated into a personal knowledge of the human condition— and "when the wind brought the sound of the great sea's voice to the men on the shore . . . they felt that they could be interpreters.". . .

As for Crane the conscious artist, [his short story] "The Monster" reminds us that he not only anticipated many of the techniques and themes of Hemingway, but that he also stands as the link between the Twain of *Pudd'nhead Wilson* and *Huckleberry Finn* and the Faulkner of *The Sound and the Fury*. The point is not simply that in *The Sound and the Fury*, as in Crane's work, a young boy is warned against "projecking" with flowers, or that Benjy is as much a "monster" as Henry Johnson, or Henry as much an idiot as Benjy, or that their communities are more monstrous than either, or that to touch either is considered a test of courage by the small fry, or even that both suffer when young white girls are frightened by them. The important point is that between Twain and the emergence of the driving honesty and social responsibility of Faulkner, no artist of Crane's caliber looked so steadily at the wholeness of American life and discovered such far-reaching symbolic equivalents for its unceasing state of civil war. Crane's work remains fresh today because he was a great artist, but perhaps he became a great artist because under conditions of pressure and panic he stuck to his guns.

Stephen Crane Is a Superior Descriptive Writer

Willa Cather

The following article is taken from the introduction to volume 9 of Wilson Follett's edition of the collected works of Stephen Crane. Entitled *Wounds in the Rain and Other Impressions of War*, the volume includes a number of short stories and sketches that Crane wrote about war. In her introduction, novelist Willa Cather assesses Crane's strengths and weaknesses, concluding that it is Crane's ability to render authentic and moving description that makes him a great writer. Cather is best known for *My Antonia*, her novel about a pioneer woman's life in the western United States.

The sketches in this volume are most of them low-pressure writing, done during, or soon after, Crane's illness in Cuba. He hadn't the vitality to make stories, to pull things together into a sharp design—though "The Price of the Harness" just misses being a fine war story. In one of them the writing is rather commonplace, the sketch "God Rest Ye, Merry Gentlemen"—the only story of Crane's I know which seems distinctly old-fashioned. It is done in an outworn manner that was considered smart in the days when Richard Harding Davis was young, and the war correspondent and his "kit" was a romantic figure. This sketch indulges in a curiously pompous kind of humour which seemed very swagger then:

"He was hideously youthful and innocent and unaware."

"Walkley departed tearlessly for Jamaica, soon after he had bestowed upon his friends much tinned goods and blankets."

"But they departed joyfully before the sun was up and passed into Siboney."

From the Introduction by Willa Cather to *The Work of Stephen Crane* by Stephen Crane, edited by Wilson Follett. Copyright ©1926 by Alfred A. Knopf Inc. Reprinted by permission of the publisher.

A COMPARISON TO KIPLING

They always departed in that school of writing, they never went anywhere. This chesty manner, doubtless, came in with Kipling. When one re-reads the young Kipling it seems a little absurd, but it still seems to belong. After it became a general affectation, however, it was surely one of the most foolish of literary fashions. But only this one of Crane's war sketches is much tainted by the war-correspondent idiom of the times. In the others he wrote better than the people of his day, and he wrote like himself. The fact that there is not much design, that these are for the most part collections of impressions which could be arranged as well in one way as another, gives one a chance to examine the sentences, which are part, but only part, of the material out of which stories are made.

When you examine the mere writing in this unorganized material, you see at once that Crane was one of the first post-impressionists; that he began it before the French painters began it, or at least as early as the first of them. He simply knew from the beginning how to handle detail. He estimated it at its true worth—made it serve his purpose and felt no further responsibility about it. I doubt whether he ever spent a laborious half-hour in doing his duty by detail––in enumerating, like an honest, grubby auctioneer. If he saw one thing that engaged him in a room, he mentioned it. If he saw one thing in a landscape that thrilled him, he put it on paper, but he never tried to make a faithful report of everything else within his field of vision, as if he were a con-scientious salesman making out his expense-account. "The red sun was pasted in the sky like a wafer," that careless ob-servation . . . isn't exceptional with Crane. (He wrote like that when he was writing well.) What about the clouds, and the light on the hills, and the background, and the fore-ground? Well, Crane left that for his successors to write, and they have been doing it ever since: accounting for every-thing, as trustees of an estate are supposed to do, thoroughly good business methods applied to art; "doing" landscapes and interiors like house-decorators, putting up the curtains and tacking down the carpets.

Perhaps it was because Stephen Crane had read so little, was so slightly acquainted with the masterpieces of fiction, that he felt no responsibility to be accurate or painstaking in accounting for things and people. He is rather the best of our writers in what is called "description" because he is the least describing. Cuba didn't tempt him to transfer tropical landscapes to paper, any more than New York State had tempted him to do his duty by the countryside.

> The day wore down to the Cuban dusk. . . . The sun threw his last lance through the foliage. The steep mountain-range on the right turned blue and as without detail as a curtain. The tiny ruby of light ahead meant that the ammunition guard were cooking their supper.

Enough, certainly. He didn't follow the movement of troops there much more literally than he had in *The Red Badge of Courage*. He knew that the movement of troops was the officers' business, not his. He was in Cuba to write about soldiers and soldiering, and he did; often something like this:

> With his heavy roll of blanket and the half of a shelter tent crossing his right shoulder and under his left arm, each man presented the appearance of being clasped from behind, wrestler-fashion, by a pair of thick white arms.

> There was something distinctive in the way they carried their rifles. There was the grace of the old hunter somewhere in it, the grace of a man whose rifle has become absolutely a part of himself. Furthermore, almost every blue shirt-sleeve was rolled to the elbow, disclosing forearms of almost incredible brawn. The rifles seemed light, almost fragile, in the hands that were at the end of those arms, never fat but always rolling with muscles and veins that seemed on the point of bursting.

That is much more to his purpose than what these men were about. That is important, all of it—and that sense of the curious smallness of rifle-butts in the hands of regulars is most important of all.

A DISLIKE OF THEATRICALITY

The most interesting things in the bundle of impressions called "War Memories" are the death of Surgeon Gibbs, Crane's observations about the regulars, "the men," and his admiration for Admiral Sampson. Sometimes when a man is writing carelessly, without the restraint he puts upon himself when he is in good form, one can surprise some of his secrets and read rather more than he perhaps intended. He admired Sampson because he wasn't like the time-honoured conception of a bluff seaman. "It is his distinction not to resemble the preconceived type of his standing. When I first met him he seemed immensely bored by the war and with the command of the North Atlantic Squadron. I perceived a manner, where I thought I perceived a mood, a point of view."

He admired the Admiral because he wasn't theatrical, detested noise and show.

> No bunting, no arches, no fireworks; nothing but the perfect management of a big fleet. That is a record for you. No trumpets, no cheers of the populace. Just plain, pure, unsauced accomplishment. But ultimately he will reap his reward in—in what? In text-books on sea campaigns. No more. The people choose their own, and they choose the kind they like. Who has a better right? Anyhow, he is a great man. And when you are once started you can continue to be a great man without the help of bouquets and banquets.

And that point of view caused Mr. Crane's biographer no little trouble. He himself managed so conspicuously to elude the banquets and bouquets of his own calling that he left a very meagre tradition among "literary people." Had he been more expansive at coffee-houses and luncheon clubs where his art was intelligently discussed, had he even talked about his own tales among a few friends, or written a few papers about his works for reviews, what a convenience for [Crane biographer] Thomas Beer! But there is every evidence that he was a reticent and unhelpful man, with no warmhearted love of giving out opinions. His ideal, apparently, was "just plain, pure, unsauced accomplishment."

Crane Is Preoccupied with the Theme of Isolation

Austin McC. Fox

Austin McC. Fox was a teacher at the Nichols School in Buffalo, New York, when he wrote this introduction to a collection of Stephen Crane short stories. McC. Fox describes what he believes to be Crane's preoccupation with the theme of isolation, an essentially twentieth-century theme that informed the work of many later writers.

Unlike William Dean Howells and Hamlin Garland, both of whom knew and encouraged him, Crane never became closely concerned with social issues. It was usually the moral or psychological aspects of a situation that caught his interest. Of his Bowery story "An Experiment in Misery" he wrote: "I tried to make plain that the root of Bowery life is a sort of cowardice. Perhaps I mean a lack of ambition or to willingly be knocked flat and accept the licking."

To this might be added a comment Crane once made: "I was a Socialist . . . but when a couple of Socialists assured me I had no right to think differently from any other Socialist and then quarrelled with each other about what Socialism meant, I ran away."

As shown by the grim description of the sweatshop and its proprietor in "Maggie," and from the comment about the Standard Oil Company at the beginning of "Virtue in War," it would probably be safe to say that Crane general sympathies were against the capitalist and clearly with the common man. . . .

THEMES

The pervading theme in Crane's stories—indeed, in all his work—is perhaps the most ubiquitous theme in all American literature: loneliness. As found in Crane, it is the loneliness of a central honest or innocent character in a situation in which he or she has to deal with worldly or morally weak people, or with an impersonal or indifferent environment. This is the situation, for example, in "Maggie," in "The Bride Comes to Yellow Sky," and in "The Pace of Youth." Maggie's drunken mother is not only a personal antagonist but also a symbol of the whole hostile and depressing world that Maggie never made. In "An Episode of War" and "The Open Boat," the opposition is clearly this indifferent and sometimes inimical world. "The Open Boat" is perhaps the most allegorical of all of Crane's stories, for it suggests that man's natural condition is one of helplessness in an open boat. The captain, the oiler, the cook, and the correspondent seem:' to stand for mankind, and the universe is represented by the ominous sea, the soaring gulls, the distant clouds and sky, the lurking sharks in the night, and the windmill on the shore:

> This tower was a giant, standing with its back to the plight of the ants. It represented in a degree, to the correspondent, the serenity of nature amid the struggles of the individual—nature in the wind, and nature in the vision of men. She did not seem cruel to him then, nor beneficent, nor treacherous, nor wise. But she was indifferent, flatly indifferent.

The story's famous opening line—"None of them knew the color of the sky"—implies that the overwhelmingness of man's struggle to survive at his own level of existence allows him little hope of any metaphysical help. Like Yeats's wild swans, the gulls become symbols of the aloofness and permanence of nature in contrast with the puniness and impermanence of man. Symbolically, too, all that the men have to help them, outside themselves, is a "thin little oar, and it seemed often ready to snap." The influence of this story, even to the oar business, on Hemingway's *The Old Man and The Sea* seems apparent.

In "An Episode of War," as the young lieutenant is dividing the coffee beans with his sword on the spread-out rubber blanket, he is, ironically, badly wounded by a stray bullet. Here again is Crane's vision of an impersonal and unpredictable world, and once again one thinks of Hemingway, this time of the scene in *A Farewell to Arms* where Lieutenant Henry and his Italian ambulance-driving friends are blown up while eating a cheese lunch. The naturalistic view of the universe in these stories and others constitutes a second major theme in Crane's work.

BRAVERY

Another major motif is Crane's almost clinical preoccupation with the behavior of men in situations of crisis or danger—both brave men and cowards figure frequently and importantly. A line-up of the courageous ones would include not only the group in "The Open Boat," the lieutenant in "An Episode of War," and Marshal Jack Potter in "The Bride Comes to Yellow Sky," but also Collins in "A Mystery of Heroism," Henry Johnson in "The Monster," the gambler in "The Blue Hotel," the New York Kid in "The Five White Mice," the Greek child in "Death and the Child," the protagonists in both "The Price of the Harness" and "Virtue in War," and a number of others. In "Death and the Child," Crane develops a child-is-father-to-the-man theory about courage, for the crawling child is unruffled by the surrounding war conditions, whereas the adult correspondent-turned-soldier, Peza, is shaken by uncontrollable fear:

> Palsied, windless and abject, he confronted the primitive courage, the sovereign child, the brother of the mountains, the sky, and the sea, and he knew that the definition of his misery could be written on a wee grass blade.

With Peza to begin a list of cowards, one can easily add some interesting others, such as the Swede and the Easterner in "The Blue Hotel," and Senator Cadogan's son, Caspar, in "The Second Generation."

From this presentation of man's conduct under crisis, however, comes perhaps the only really positive and hopeful note in Crane's writing. This is not based simply on the argument that the brave men far outnumber the cowards. It rests mainly on a clear affirmation, which sounds throughout most of his stories, of man's occasional capacity for courage and endurance.

A fourth major theme is the very ironic one that generosity often leads to suffering. This is found, for example, in "The Monster," when Dr. Trescott's deeply felt moral obligation to save the life of the Negro hired man Henry Johnson, who has rescued his son, leads to his ostracism in his home town. The narrowness and conformity of small-town life and the maliciousness of feminine gossip, although lesser themes in this and other of the Whilomville stories, point up the influence of Crane on such later American provincial realists as Sinclair Lewis and Sherwood Anderson.

One also finds in Crane variations on the father-and-son theme, or more specifically as applied to Crane, the mother-and-daughter or father-and-daughter motif. This occupies a large place in "Maggie," "The Pace of Youth," and "The Second Generation." In any of its forms it pivots on the inability of two different generations to understand each other.

A final theme to comment on is the children-are-a-race-apart one. In this Crane aligns himself with the Mark Twain of *Tom Sawyer*, and clearly anticipates Booth Tarkington; indeed, Penrod and his pals seem to be fashioned almost directly after Jimmie Trescott and his friends in "Angel Child" and the other Whilomville stories in which they appear. Particularly, the nauseating Lola Pratt of Tarkington's *Seventeen* seems to be descended directly from the Angel Child herself.

IMAGERY AND SYMBOLISM

Of all Crane's qualities as a writer, it is, I think, his metaphorical imagination that most impresses the reader. Again and again one is struck by some particularly vivid piece of imagery. At times the image may lean toward theatricality, but much more often it will be arresting, perceptive, and original, yet effectively understated. Here, for instance, is Marshal Jack Potter riding self-consciously in a Texas railroad coach alongside his new bride on their way home to Yellow Sky:

> He sat with a hand on each knee, like a man waiting in a barber's shop.

And thus Crane sees the tents of American soldiers in the Spanish-American War for "The Price of the Harness":

> Here were scattered tiny white shelter tents, and in the darkness they were luminous like the rearing stones in a graveyard.

And the scene in the Bowery tale called "George's Mother," as George Kelcey is reluctantly on his way to the prayer meeting with his mother:

> In a dark street the little chapel sat humbly between two towering apartment houses. A red street damp stood in front. It threw a marvelous reflection upon the wet pavements. It was like the death stain of a spirit.

This juxtaposing of purity and worldliness seems to be a deliberate part of Crane's literary method, not only in such descriptions as this, but in putting side by side such opposite characters as Maggie and her mother, or the timid, newly married Mrs. Jack Potter and the blustering, drunken Scratchy Wilson in "The Bride Comes to Yellow Sky." This is the ironic nature of things, Crane seems to say, and this, one cannot help noticing, is the source of much of the ironic power of his stories. The good and innocent often suffer, and tragedy ensues, continues Crane, because neither Providence nor the guilty bystanders in the world will intercede. This, I think, is the meaning of Crane's direct statement to the reader at the end of "The Blue Hotel."

Often it is the opening description in Crane's stories that strikes the note of the indifference of the universe, and swirling dust, rain, snow, or fog becomes a symbol of this indifference. It is a blizzard in "Men in the Storm," rain in "An Experiment in Misery," fog in "The Little Regiment" (it was fog, too, in *The Red Badge of Courage*), and dust at the beginning of part two of "Maggie":

> A wind of early autumn raised yellow dust from cobbles and swirled it against a hundred windows.

Again the Hemingway reader will notice a similarity.

Although Crane changes his color symbolism from time to time, he generally seems to use yellows in unpleasant associations. Here, in "The Second Generation," he uses yellow to emphasize death and revulsion:

> In and out of the ditchlike trenches lay the Spanish dead, lemon-faced corpses. . . .

Stallman has spoken of Crane's extraordinary preoccupation with blue. Beer mentions his "passion for red," and states that his "purple was sinister and repugnant." Berryman has also commented on his colors. In "The Open Boat," gray is the keynote color—in the sky, the gulls, the sea, and the faces—and contributes much to the impersonal-universe theme of the story.

Other symbolic possibilities about which one cannot help speculating are the frequent games of chance in Crane's stories, used as devices for pointing up the absence of moral purpose in the world—the dice game in "The Five White Mice," and the card game in "The Blue Hotel," for instance. Then there is the circus in "The Five White Mice," the carousel in "The Pace of Youth," and the dime museum with its "meek freaks" in "Maggie." All seem somehow to strengthen the feeling of the world's lack of moral direction or divine organization.

ALLEGORY

It is not difficult to see many symbols in Crane's writing. Occasionally these symbols will carry the whole story into the deeper realm of allegory. In "The Open Boat" one has such a story. Perhaps one finds another in "The Pace of Youth," with its symbolic pursuit of the young lovers by the middle-aged father. In this collection there are others, too, which offer intriguing allegorical possibilities.

NARRATIVE METHOD

Crane builds his stories around a single mood, to which, as one can see, his use of colors contributes. In his longer narratives, however, he may have a series of moods, which he indicates by separations in the text. Often his stories end with a small piece of action quietly pointing out the ironic truth contained in the story, as when Dr. Trescott at the end of "The Monster" is shown absently counting all the unused teacups of the ladies who have stayed away from his wife's tea party.

STYLE

There are details about Crane's writing style that one would have otherwise: his strong predilection, for instance, for the passive voice, the split infinitive, and the misplaced adverb. Lack of good formal training? Indifference? Haste? In any case, it was part of the man and therefore part of the writer. Regarding his general writing style, perhaps the best comment has come from another professional story writer, Willa Cather:

> When you examine the mere writing in this unorganized material [Crane's war sketches], you see at once that Crane was one of the first post-impressionists; that he began it before the French painters began it, or at least as early as the first of them. He simply knew from the beginning how to handle detail He estimated it at its true worth—made it serve his purpose and felt no further responsibility about it I doubt whether he ever spent a laborious half-hour in doing his duty by detail—in enumerating, like an honest, grubby auctioneer. If he saw one thing that engaged him in a room, he mentioned it. If he saw one thing in a landscape that thrilled him, he put it on paper, but he never tried to make a faithful report of everything else within his field of vision, as if he were a conscientious salesman making out his expense-account. "The red sun was pasted in the sky like a wafer," that careless observation which Mr. Hergesheimer admires so much, isn't exceptional with Crane. (He wrote like that when he was

writing well.) What about the clouds, and the light on the hills, and the background, and the foreground? Well, Crane left that for his successors to write, and they have been doing it ever since: accounting for everything, as trustees of an estate are supposed to do. . . .

EVALUATION OF CRANE'S STORIES

Originating with Irving and Poe, the short story in America has had some distinguished practitioners—Hawthorne, Bret Harte, Mark Twain, Henry James, Jack London, Ring Lardner, Fitzgerald, Hemingway, Faulkner, Salinger, and a goodly number of others. Curiously, it is difficult to recall more than three to six of the stories of any one of the writers in this genre which are particularly well remembered or to which one can give the highest rating. This situation suggests inconsistency of performance, or a reluctance on the part of readers and critics to recognize much more than each writer's very best. Three of the stories in the group that follows—"The Open Boat," "The Bride Comes to Yellow Sky," and "The Blue Hotel"—have come to be ranked with the best our short-story tradition has produced.

Crane Is a Literary Impressionist

James Nagel

Critic James Nagel has studied the subject of impressionism—in literature, music, and art—for many years. Awarded a Fulbright Lectureship at the University of Waikato in Hamilton, New Zealand, Nagel taught a graduate seminar on Stephen Crane and Ernest Hemingway, where he took an interest in Crane and impressionism. In the following article, Nagel argues that Crane's style, which is episodic rather than continuous, and the fact that he seems uninterested in defining reality, is essentially impressionistic. Although Crane includes naturalism and realism in his works, Nagel believes that neither of these descriptions really categorizes his work.

Literary Impressionism is more than an occasional tendency in Crane's fiction; it is the continuing and informing concept of both art and theme throughout his works. It has a direct bearing on his central themes and methods from his earliest stories through his major works to his final novel. The norms of Impressionism provide a context in which his narrative methods, themes, characterizations, images, and structural devices can be perceived as part of a holistic aesthetic behind nearly everything he wrote.

But Impressionism is not the only impulse visible in Crane's fiction. His work embraces a wide range of literary tendencies. The occasional use of personification as a device of characterization, and of zeugma as figure, reveal studied Classical tendencies. The suggestion of spiritualism in nature implies Romanticism and Transcendentalism, although Crane's use of this idea is decidedly limited. There are Genteel elements in the romance plots of *Active Service* and *The Third Violet* and some of the short stories, such as "The Grey Sleeve." Indeed, as Daniel G. Hoffman has said, "Crane was

Reprinted from James Nagel, *Stephen Crane and Literary Impressionism* (University Park: Pennsylvania State University Press). Copyright ©1980 by The Pennsylvania State University (now reverted to the author). Reprinted by permission of the author.

a literary chameleon, writing in almost every fashion then prevailing: naturalism, impressionism, psychological realism, local color, native humor." But the only two movements, other than Impressionism, that have played a significant role in his fiction are Naturalism and Realism. . . .

Although there is virtually nothing Naturalistic about *The Red Badge of Courage* and most of Crane's other works, there are definite Naturalistic tendencies in some of his stories, especially in the Bowery tales. Crane's inscription in Hamlin Garland's copy of *Maggie* to the effect that "environment is a tremendous thing in the world and frequently shapes lives regardless" expresses an awareness of sociological determinism, although it inadequately describes the events of the novel. The boys of the opening chapter "fighting in the modes of four thousand years ago" provide direct textual evidence of Naturalistic ideas, as do the Bowery setting of the novel, the degraded characters, the tone of their lives, and the generalized feeling that life is a hopeless struggle.

These kinds of ideas appear in nearly all of the Bowery tales, sometimes with savage force. Surely "A Dark-Brown Dog," in which a father throws his son's dog out a window to his death, develops a sense of devastating degradation. Other of these stories, including "An Ominous Baby" and "A Great Mistake," portray the debased human condition of this environment. A largely ignored story, "The Snake," contains a direct indication of genetic Darwinism. As a man encounters a deadly snake in the wild, the narrator explains the man's instinctive reaction: "In the man was all the wild strength of the terror of his ancestors, his race, of his kind. A deadly repulsion had been handed from man to man through long dim centuries." Later, as he seizes a stick and smashes the snake to death, "the man went sheer raving mad from the emotions of his fore-fathers and from his own." The Bowery environment is a significant motivational impulse in *George's Mother*, as it is in *Maggie*, especially if the term "environment" means not only things and persons but attitudes and ideas as well.

NATURALISM

Of the stories with Naturalistic elements, perhaps the finest are "The Men in the Storm" and "An Experiment in Misery." "The Men in the Storm" portrays Nature as a cognitively hostile entity lashing out at men who wait to enter a soup kitchen. The men are debased and hopeless; social injustice and callousness have turned them into passive sheep; their expressions suggest that they "were trying to perceive where they had failed, what they had lacked, to be thus vanquished in the race." "An Experiment in Misery" develops similar themes of social injustice, suggesting social pathology in the lives of derelicts who, stripped of clothing and other indicators of economic status, stand "massively, like chiefs." Their deficiencies do not emerge until they don their clothing and once again assume a definable role in society.

If Naturalism plays a role in these stories in the portrayal of the lower classes a hostile Nature, and genetic and economic determinism, it is ultimately inadequate as a term to describe Crane's works in general. Epistemological processes are far more important than deterministic forces, Nature is more often indifferent or inscrutable than hostile, free will plays a more important role than either chance or fate. Nearly every aspect of artistic methodology points toward Impressionism rather than Naturalism, even in the Bowery tales. Moreover, Crane's use of irony in all of his important works is patently discordant with Naturalism, which most often grinds on with steadfast seriousness toward the revelation of tragic inevitability. Even those scholars who regard Crane as a Naturalist are forced to admit that the dominant unifying element in his work is not the exercise of inexorable destiny but the ironic and problematic disparity between truth and illusion, between "nature in the wind, and nature in the vision of men."

In Naturalism reality is stable, known, and analyzed to reveal its causal forces. There is no interpretive disparity to create a basis for irony. On the other hand, the uncertainties of Impressionism, its apprehensional difficulties and its stress on the relativity of points of view, create a constant ironic interplay of varying perceptions of reality. Given these polarities, Crane's works almost invariably belong in the Impressionistic ledger. As R.W. Stallman has said, "irony is Crane's chief technical instrument." There is an ironic disparity at the heart of Crane's work, some distortion or paradox or misinterpretation that gives the narrative an ironic impulse beyond the bare structure of events. The most frequent source of such irony is false estimate of self, a disproportional sense of stature that often leads to a climactic scene of diminution. In effect, Crane's Impressionistic method makes ironic what in Naturalism would be tragic. In Crane's work deflation brings a character into confrontation with reality, however uncomfortable, and may equip the slighted character to better grapple with the world around him. In Naturalism deflation beneath the crushing forces of socioeconomic deprivation would be overwhelming, resulting in a totally defeated, defenseless character. In this sense *Maggie* and *George's Mother* may contain elements of Naturalism, but *The Red Badge*, the Sullivan County tales, Crane's potboiler novels, and the bulk of the stories certainly do not. . . .

REALISM

Crane's works are almost anti-Naturalistic, especially artistically. Naturalism tends toward epic scope in length and focus; Crane's works consist of episodic units of extreme brevity. Naturalism employs an omniscient narrator who, in largely expository passages, analyzes the themes of the narrative: Crane's works utilize a restricted narrative stance which projects the interpretations of the characters and eschews authorial comment. . . . Naturalism forces its characters into the common lot, into a condition shared by other members of the group; Crane's Impressionism, with its stress on unique sensory evocations and personal interpretation of experience, tends toward isolation, individuality, discrete human personalities. Any businessman could become George Hurstwood, any downtrodden farmer Sam Lewiston, but there will only be one Henry Fleming, one Professor Wainwright, one George Kelcey, one Maggie. For all of these reasons, Crane's works must ultimately be viewed as containing elements of Naturalism in selected works but also as having more significant attributes in both theme and technique which are directly counter to Naturalistic norms.

Realism plays a much more significant role in Crane's fiction on nearly all levels. One problem in determining the extent to which Realism functions in Crane's works is that it is difficult to postulate clear distinctions between it and Impressionism in many areas. For example, both movements employ similar characters, common folk drawn from middle-America and portrayed in everyday situations. If Crane's characters have this in common with Realism, there are also some aspects of his methods of characterization that have a different emphasis. Although both Realism and Im-

CRANE IS NOT A REALIST

Although Stephen Crane's fiction is often described as "realism" (especially in literary histories), the term is inappropriate and misleading. It is inevitably applied, however, for Crane was doing his major work during the years when realism, under the powerful sponsorship of William Dean Howells, was sweeping the field in American fiction. And like the realists, Crane chose certain characteristic subjects and themes—slum life, war, prostitution, and alcoholism—and insisted upon the freedom to treat them from unorthodox points of view. In this limited sense he is a realist.

But, Crane's fiction is radically different from that of the realists, and this difference, carefully considered, helps us to grasp the special significance of his work. At bottom his sense of reality is quite apart from those of, say, Norris, Dreiser, Garland, and Twain; for when Crane *sees* something—an object, event, or person—he does not assume (as they do) that it is a fixed, definable, irreducible fact that would carry the same meaning for any normal, truthful observer. To Crane, reality was; complex, ambivalent, ambiguous, and elusive, as much a matter of the play of a peculiarity of mind as of a quality or character in the object itself. This the reader must constantly bear in mind if he is to avoid the errors of those who complain that his fiction lacks "realistic" authority, is irrational, inconsistent, and illogical. . . .

These stories and novels are representative of Crane's art at its best. It is not the art of the realist but of an impressionist, and one is not surprised that Crane, living in a time when literary realism was drawing its practitioners from the ranks of journalists, was never successful as a newspaper reporter. He could not, as Howells was advocating, represent the world as it "actually is"; in his best work he transformed the mere appearance of things into the poetry of impressionism, and when he was good, as he often was, revealed the inner reality of the world he observed.

James B. Colvert, introduction to *Great Short Works of Stephen Crane.* New York: Harper & Row, 1968.

pressionism use objective narrative methods, Realistic works have somewhat more access to information derived from sources beyond empirical data. As a result, a Realistic narrator is likely to know the names of the characters; an Impressionistic narrator often does not. Biographical background is more important in Realism than in Impressionism, and Realistic works often provide such information directly or devise a dramatic method for its revelation. But even here the methods and efforts can be similar. In *The Rise of Silas Lapham*, for instance, Howells provides an account of Silas' early financial rise through the strategy of having Bartley Hubbard interview him for the "Solid Man of Boston" series in *The Events*. The reader gets not only the facts of the case but Hubbard's cynical view of their stereotypic and melodramatic qualities as well. Crane deals with his character's previous life a bit more subtly in *The Red Badge* by placing Henry in a situation of uncertainty and stress in which he might naturally review the events that brought him into the war, especially if these memories recall a more secure period in his life. As his regiment becomes more involved in the fighting, it becomes quite clear that Henry "wished without reserve that he was at home again." But there are not sharp disparities between these methodologies.

Differences in the roles the characters play, however, do offer some lines of determination. This point is not clear in simple "slice of life" Realism, which closely resembles Impressionism, but it is somewhat more distinct in Realistic works that culminate in moral crisis for the central character, as do *Silas Lapham, A Modern Instance*, and a host of other works by Howells, along with Twain's *Huckleberry Finn*, Cable's *The Grandissimes*, James' *The American*, and other prototypical works. Such climactic scenes function in Realism because the protagonist understands reality well enough to be able to ponder a complex choice of alternatives. But ethical issues are incapable of resolution in Impressionistic works in which the central character is struggling to perceive reality and in which his grasp of circumstances is inchoate. Thus little drama is involved in his choice of one course of action over another. In such works, some alteration of perception is sufficient to provide a climax, a problem certainly anterior to any capacity for meaningful moral decisions. In this sense the themes and plots of Impressionism are more primitive, occur earlier in the epistemological process, than those of Realism. The irreducible norm of Realism is that reality is known and recorded: this assumption is not certain in Impressionism. As a result, Realism concentrates more on determining what to do about reality, Impressionism more on attempting to define and understand it.

Within these polarities, Crane's fiction is decidedly Impressionistic rather than Realistic. Although many of his works touch on various ethical matters, very few of them use a moral crisis as a climactic moment. Far more of them have as a central scene some key juncture in the growth of a character in which something is realized, perceived in a new way, or not perceived when it should have been. For example, in "The Open Boat" the correspondent's realization that Nature is indifferent and that he is, as an individual, insignificant in the universe, provides the intellectual climax of the story, just as the arrival on shore constitutes a resolution of the adventure plot. The same kind of climax is at the crux of *The Red Badge, George's Mother, The Monster,* "The Blue Hotel" and "The Bride Comes to Yellow Sky," while *Maggie* offers a case in which much might have been realized by Maggie, her mother, Jimmie, and Pete, but is not. Here the perceptual themes culminate in vacuity, opacity, blindness; the central ethical questions are evaded rather than confronted by the characters.

IMPRESSIONISM

There are also some structural distinctions between Realism and Impressionism which help place Crane in the latter category. There is no injunction for brevity in Realism; since reality is known, it can be represented as a continuum of experience, reasonably stable, certain, comprehensible. On the other hand, in Impressionism reality is in rapid flux: Claude Monet's haystacks are very different when viewed at varying times of the day, even when seen from the same perspective. To portray Impressionistic reality, therefore, episodes must be brief, capturing discrete moments of experience in which the world is perceived and internalized but not arrested, touched for an instant but not known for all time. In this regard Crane's works, with few exceptions, such as *The O'Ruddy,* are emphatically Impressionistic, tending toward aggregates of episodes rather than continuous action. There is little distinction here between the structural units of the short stories and these of the novels: both tend to be composed of episodes of a few pages strung together by continuities of character and place but not of action. There is rarely a story that proceeds from beginning to end with no lapses in chronology, no breaks between scenes. Nor does Crane characteristically provide expository links to explain what happened between episodes; scenes begin and end abruptly, often commencing with visual descriptions of the environment and concluding in the midst of action or dialogue. No attempt is made to circumscribe reality, to give it full definition.

If there is a sense in which Crane must be described as a Realist, beyond historic considerations, it is in his portrayal of the mental flow of his characters. Crane was not a psychological Realist in the Jamesean sense in that he did not portray with any sophistication the major psychological theories of the day, unique aberrations of thought or feeling, extraordinary psychic trauma. Indeed, what is compelling about the mental lives of his major figures is their normality. Fleming's guilt and fear, Maggie's romantic longings, George Kelcey's love-hate relationship with his mother, are all of the most ordinary sort. Crane's psychological "realism" is notable as an epistemological record of sensory experience, followed by internalization, reflection, fantasy. It is the very commonality of this process, the "truth" of it, which gives the sense of being real.

Certainly there is a dramatic psychological realism in *The Red Badge* which overpowers any dimension of historical scene. The Bowery of *Maggie* is somewhat more present in the rich description of saloon halls and grimy tenements, but it is ultimately the mental distortions of the principal characters that carry the most force. The same thing is true of Crane's portrayal of the West in "A Man and Some Others," "The Bride Comes to Yellow Sky," and "The Blue Hotel." "The Open Boat" eschews the realistic physical detail of the journalistic sketch "Stephen Crane's Own Story" to focus more intently on the thought and emotional development of the correspondent. Even Crane's journalism shows much more gift for psychological process than for descriptive detail.

Ultimately, then, Crane can be considered a Realist in only a qualified sense. His work shares with the norms of American Realism a rejection of many of the tendencies of Romanticism, including stylistic elevation, transcendental metaphysics and pantheism, symbolization, allegorical plots and characters, and a general inclination to represent people and events as emblematic of a significance beyond themselves. As did most realists, Crane portrayed ordinary people who spoke in the vernacular and confronted situations drawn from within a common range. But unlike the Realists, Crane depicted an unstable, changing world in the process of being perceived. Things "seem" to be a certain way in Crane; they "are" in Realism.

Viewed in totality, and with regard for both craft and meaning, Crane's fiction exceeds the limits of both Realism and Naturalism and ultimately must be described and interpreted as being essentially Impressionistic. When seen from this perspective, the Crane canon, and the major phases within his work, reveal a rather different writer, and a rather different contribution, than has generally been recorded in modern scholarship. . . .

CRANE'S INFLUENCE

It is precisely Crane's Impressionistic tendencies which form his most significant influence on the twentieth century and which evoke the Modernistic tone of his fiction. His objective mode of presentation and ability to portray tragedy with understated emotion are a dramatic foreshadowing of what would become hallmarks of the style of Ernest Hemingway. A paragraph in "Crane at Velestino," one report in Crane's journalistic coverage of the Greco-Turkish war, is a characteristic example:

> I noticed one lieutenant standing up in the rear of a trench rolling a cigarette, his legs wide apart. In this careless attitude a shot went through his neck. His servant came from the trench and knelt weeping over the body, regardless of the battle. The men had to drag him in by the legs.

But the most influential single work in American literature to grow out of the origins of Impressionism in the 1890s was clearly *The Red Badge of Courage.* It was the first American Impressionistic novel to attain widespread popular attention in both Europe and the United States. Although the reviews of it were mixed, partly out of confusion about its methodology, it quickly won critical acclaim. It was described variously as a battle painting, a montage of photographs, a verbal record that permitted the reader to "see" the action. Behind it were Crane's years as a struggling journalist with an eye for detail and an ear for irony, his experience with young painters in the Art Student's League, his untiring attempts to write true to his own vision and in his own style. From *The Red Badge* and the works surrounding it there radiates an enormous and generally misunderstood influence on American letters. . . .

[Crane's] work is sparse, crisp, sensory; there is no authorial presence, little unobserved description and even less judgment, and few wasted words. The ultimate impact of his work is aesthetic. There is little call to social action, no program of economic reform, and rarely a word of popular social theory. . . .

The aesthetics of Crane's Impressionism, especially its anti-didacticism and art-for-art's sake implications, bear some similarities to such recent developments as Sur-Fiction in the United States. The recognition of Crane's role as an Impressionist is thus a crucial determinant of his place in cultural history.

The significance of Crane's achievement has not been totally ignored, even though it has been widely misinterpreted, by literary scholarship. Both Vernon Louis Parrington and Fred Lewis Pattee proclaimed him to be the genius of his decade. Carl Van Doren, writing in 1924, maintained that Modern American literature began with the work of Crane. Looking back in 1926, Joseph Conrad wrote that in Crane "we had an artist, a man not of experience but a man inspired, a seer with a gift for rendering the significant on the surface of things. . . ." And Conrad was joined by Edward Garnett in declaring Crane to be the leading Impressionist of his time. The enthusiastic interest in Crane's fiction that emerged in the 1920s, and the enormous attention paid to his life and work in modern scholarship, attest to the continuing value of his contribution, a contribution that is fundamentally and inextricably part of the development of Literary Impressionism.

Crane's Work Criticizes Society

Russel B. Nye

In the following article, critic Russel B. Nye argues
that much of Crane's work attempted to define social
problems and offer solutions. Nye points out that
Crane spent much of his life living among the poor
and destitute, and concludes that he had plenty of time
to study problems and use them as an inspiration.

The wave of humanitarianism and social reform which
swept over the United States after the post-Appomattox
period of expansion encompassed in its breadth some
widely disassociated strains of thought. A crusade against a
laissez-faire philosophy materialized in religious, political,
economic, and social thought, and the last quarter of the old
century saw sharply defined groups of liberal and conservative set one against the other. The historical significance of
the liberal movement of the 1890's, and its effects in literature and socio-political thought, need no review or interpretation here. The opponents of the individualistic, Spencerian
doctrine, numbering among them the familiar names of
Howells, Bellamy, Garland, Riis, Woolsey, Root, La Follette,
Henry George, Veblen, many others in equally widely dis-
tributed fields, criticized in one way or another existing conditions, each attempting to find a more or less collectivistic
way out of a naturalistic chaos. The attention of thinkers in
every field was turned toward society, and literature too
began to take on social meaning. We do not ordinarily classify Stephen Crane among these social critics, but his interest in poverty, crime, maladjustment, and other problems of
an urban society, led him, as well, to search for a solution to
the social riddle.

Critics of Crane seem to have agreed upon two aspects of
his mind and art worth emphasis, his technical contribu-
tions to the short story, and his naturalistic philosophy. Both

Reprinted from Russel B. Nye, "Stephen Crane as Social Critic," *Modern Quarterly*,
Summer 1940, by permission of the author's estate.

of these approaches to Crane are real and valuable, but there seems to have been more or less overlooked what is perhaps the essential portion of his work, that is, his social thought and criticism, his extreme awareness of life around him, his consciousness of a class struggle. A great deal of attention has been paid to Crane's realistic method, but little to what problems he presented realistically—the problems of society.

This sociological interest on Crane's part is evident in numerous incidents given by Thomas Beer in his biography of the man. Crane talked sympathetically and interestedly to New York streetwalkers, wandered through the Bowery, slept in flophouses, talked with drifters, pried stories out of breadlines and loiterers, and kept himself out of money by responding too readily to a hard luck story. Crane knew the lower levels of New York life as well as, if not better than, any other literary man of his day. This social consciousness is a major portion of his interest and of his art, one which we cannot afford to overlook.

Around this interest in and observation of society, Stephen Crane built an important part of his work. His novels and novelettes, *The Red Badge of Courage, Active Service, The O'Ruddy, The Third Violet,* and his war sketches, *Tales of Two Wars, Wounds in the Rain,* are no doubt familiar to many readers. A survey of his interest in the submerged tenth, however, of his interest in the Bowery he knew, opens an area comparatively unexplored.

Maggie

It is significant that Crane's first book, *Maggie, A Girl of the Streets,* 1893, deals with a social problem. What are the causes, he argues, which lie behind delinquency? The sweatshop, poverty, society and its false standards, tenement life—these things, all remediable by intelligent reform, cause Maggie's fall. In nearly all of the *Midnight Sketches, An Experiment in Misery, A Street Scene in New York, A Self-Made Man, An Ominous Baby, The Monster, The Auction, George's Mother, Whilomville Stories, A Desertion,* and a few others, we find the continuation in prose of his discussion of the problems which lay before him in society.

An Experiment in Misery Crane wrote after spending a night in a Bowery flophouse. A youth, standing penniless in the city, sees a multitude of buildings, of pitiless hues and sternly high, emblematic of a nation forcing its regal head into the clouds, throwing no downward glances; in the sublimity of its aspirations ignoring the wretches who flounder at its feet.

. . . social position, comfort, the pleasures of living, were unconquerable kingdoms.

Representative of an impersonal and unheeding society, the city wrings from him

the protest of the wretch who feels the touch of the imperturbable granite wheels, and who then cries with an impersonal eloquence, with a strength not from him, giving voice to the wail of a whole section, a class, a people.

OTHER STORIES

In the face of this terrible and impersonal cruelty of society, weak men quail, and this lack of courage, this giving up of personal aim, is to Crane one great cause of social illness. Courage, then, is one answer, but it. is not the complete solution to the problem of social dereliction. Aside from the personal equation, and what is more important, society in the aggregate must reform and realign itself. In the series called *Midnight Sketches*, Crane, with his scrupulous honesty, set down conditions as he saw them in lower New York, conditions which intelligent reform and social rehabilitation could easily wipe out. Not only is institutional reform needed, but a revolution in social psychology. In *The Monster*, as has but been pointed out, Crane attacks the hypocrisy and injustice of the mob mind, choosing as its most representative figure the gossipy, small-minded old maid. The cruelty of society to the individual indicated to Crane that psychological as well as institutional reform was necessary for society.

Turning once more to the personal equation in society, Crane wrote *George's Mother*, in which lack of opportunity, lack of initiative, and, ironically enough, mother-love, combine to replace a young man's ambition with frustration and defeat—the defeatism and cowardice which Crane saw as an important cause of the individual's maladjustment to society. This story and *An Experiment in Misery* may be bracketed together as studies in the evolution of a Broadway drifter.

The closest approach found in Crane's work to economic criticism as a part of social theory appears in the stories *A Self-Made Man* and *An Ominous Baby*. The former is a satiric sketch of a man's rise in the world, while the latter, upon closer examination, gives an important key to this aspect of his social thinking. Given two children, the one poor, the other rich and pampered. The child of wealth has a toy which the other desires, so the poor child takes it by force and runs away. How shall we interpret the act of this *ominous* child? Is Crane here merely placing in simple terms an argument for a more equal distribution of wealth and property? Is he advocating or anticipating a class revolt? Some such interpretation is fairly clear—at least he tomes perilously close to an almost anarchistic conception of a solution for economic inequality.

The interest in children displayed in *An Ominous Baby* Crane carried into his *Whilomville Stories.* Rather than being humorous sketches, these stories are significant in an analysis of his social thought. Crane studied the world of the child

PEOPLE AS THEY SEEM TO ME

In a November 1896 letter to a fan, Catherine Harris, Crane explains about his reasons for writing Maggie.

Thank you very much for your letter on Maggie. I will try to answer your questions properly and politely. . . . I have spent a great deal of time on the East Side and that I have no opinion of missions. That—to you—may not be a valid answer since perhaps you have been informed that I am not very friendly to Christianity as seen around town. I do not think that much can be done with the Bowery as long as the [*word blurred*] are in their present state of conceit. A person who thinks himself superior to the rest of us because he has no job and no pride and no clean clothes is as badly conceited. . . . In a story of mine called "An Experiment in Misery" I tried to make plain that the root of Bowery life is a sort of cowardice. Perhaps I mean a lack of ambition or to willingly be knocked flat and accept the licking. The missions for children are another thing and if you will have Mr. Rockefeller give me a hundred street cars and some money I will load all the babes off to some pink world where cows can lick their noses and they will never see their families any more. My good friend Edward Townsend—have you read his "Daughter of the Tenements"?—has another opinion of the Bowery and it is certain to be better than mine. I had no other purpose in writing "Maggie" than to show people to people as they seem to me. If that be evil make the most of it.

because it contained in little the world of adults; the child's society was to him a microcosmic representation of the greater society he probed in his other stories; it was man's society reduced to simplest terms, with all the ills of that society present in miniature. How did these things come to be in children? was Crane's question—are social ills and their causes born in man? No, he feels, they develop only as the child begins to merge his individuality with the greater pattern of society as the individual clashes with the group. Man is not innately evil; he rather learns and adopts. This, I think, is the real social significance of the *Whilomville Stories*, that in them Crane is searching in the child's society for the answers to the questions of an adult society. They seem to show that the origin of social evil is without rattler shall within mankind, and thus may be escaped.

After a survey of Crane's social thought, we are faced with a seeming contradiction, a lack of alignment, in his larger philosophy. How can the dichotomy between social reform and humanitarianism on the one hand, and a naturalistic fatalism on the other as expressed in *The Open Boat* and *The Red Badge of Courage*, be explained? If we live in a universe of blind forces, how call we hope to better man's condition in society when we are at the mercy of these forces beyond our power to control? The answer is, of course, that Crane was not wholly a naturalist. He did not let a naturalistic view of the universe lead him into an amoral social philosophy of survival of the fittest, of life as a state of war on the social level. It is important to note that he at no time condoned the Frank Cowperwoods, the Wolf Larsens, or the Jadwins of his day. The cleavage in Crane's philosophy seemingly is explained thus: the forces of destiny are blind and impersonal and cannot be conquered, as we see in *The Open Boat;* but the forces of society, those which lead to the social evil seen in *Maggie* and other of his stories, are man-made forces, and can be controlled by man, who set them in motion. The world of nature we can only fate with stoicism; the world of society, however, call be reshaped—progress is possible on the human and social level. The individual, then, Crane feels, must adjust himself to two spheres of life, nature and society. In relation to the former he is powerless; his relation to the latter ought to be one of humanitarianism, tolerance, and justice. He seems to feel that man in the aggregate, after his individuality has been lost in the crowd, is cruel, or rather, needlessly inhumane and unintelligent. If men will try to improve, both individually and collectively, as they are free to do so, their social state, and if they will avoid the hypocrisy and cowardice which lie at the root of social evil, the world and its society will be a better place in which to live. This is, in essence, the core of Stephen Crane's social philosophy, ideas which place him as a critic squarely in the liberal realistic, humanitarian tradition of his day.

EVIL

Crane's conceptions of evil, freewill, and progress perhaps need further clarification and summary. As previously explained, freewill and progress are co-existent on the social human level, but not existent in relation to the forces of outside, physical nature. Evil, to Crane, seems to mean specifically social evil, as in the stories already discussed which evil finds its origin not in individual man but in institutions, in society (which is man collectively), in the friction which arises from the necessity of individualities living in relation with one another. Reform, rehabilitation, and a new system of social ethics and psychology can of course avert this type of evil. On the other hand, there intrudes often into man's society the forces of nature, causing incidents which can more easily be called fatalistic than evil, since the naturalistic physical world knows neither good nor evil nor volition. Here, of course, there is neither escape nor solution as we see in *The Open Boat* and *The Blue Hotel.* This latter story, when contrasted with *Maggie*, illustrates this double aspect of evil especially well. The death of the Swede is the logical result of a series of happenings which were harmless in themselves. It is caused by fate the blind force of a naturalistic universe, which ill this case has invaded the world of society. Nothing could have been done to avert this culmination or collaboration of events. But the death of Maggie, conversely, was not such—her end is the result of a set of social conditions, remediable and removable by society. In the world of man, then, natural law need not hold completely, and the suicides of future Maggies can be averted. To study and observe these conditions, and to find perhaps a solution, was the objective of Stephen Crane's social criticism.

Crane's View of Women

Carol Hurd Green

Carol Hurd Green is associate dean of arts and sciences at Boston College. Green's interests in addition to Stephen Crane include women and politics of the 1960s and social reformer Dorothy Day. In the following article, Green argues that Crane's female characters leave something to be desired: They betray men, are self-righteous, and care little for others.

Stephen Crane, who died at twenty-eight, was always a young writer. Nowhere is his youth more apparent than in his attitude toward women. In a letter to an early love, Nellie Crouse, he wrote of himself:

> So you think I am successful? Well I don't know. Most people consider me successful. At least, they seem to so think. But upon my soul I have lost all appetite for victory, as victory is defined by the mob. I will be glad if I can feel on my death-bed that my life has been just and kind according to my ability and that every particle of my little ridiculous stock of eloquence and wisdom has been applied for the benefit of my kind. From this moment to that death-bed may be a short time or a long one but at any rate it means a life of labor and sorrow. I do not confront it blithely. I confront it with desperate resolution. . . . I do not expect to do good. But I expect to make a sincere, desperate, lonely battle to remain true to my conception of my life. . . . It is not a fine prospect. I only speak of it to people in whose opinions I have faith. No woman has heard it until now.

The tone is stylishly world-weary, the voice that of an eager, appealing, and literary self-absorbed youth whose infatuation with himself is clear. He professes himself infatuated as well with Nellie, but the measure of his regard is in the assurance that she is worthy of his confidence.

In Crane's poetry and fiction, such self-absorption and high intentions leave women out of serious consideration; they are never more than images. And the images are those

Excerpted from Carol Hurd Green, "Stephen Crane and the Fallen Women," in *American Novelists Revisited: Essays in Feminist Criticism*, edited by Fritz Fleischmann (Boston: G.K. Hall, 1982). Reprinted by permission of the author.

seen from a perspective of adolescence: women are mothers or crabby-teacher figures or gossips, sexless and shapeless, manufacturing and exerting authority, or—if they are young and shapely—seductresses, or (like Grace Fanhall in *The Third Violet*) the stuff of which romantic dreams are made. In the presence of women, men are driven to nonsense, silence, impotence, or guilt. Women, too, fall prey to members of their own sex; there is not among them the loyalty of brotherhood that Crane, the "preacher's kid," created as a faith. It was that capacity for loyalty that redeemed men; without it, all women—not just the prostitutes who fascinated Crane—were fallen women. . . .

WOMEN IN CRANE'S POETRY

Like the fiction, Crane's poetry pays relatively little attention to women; Crane's imagination functions best in the world of men. When the poetry does concentrate on women, it reveals a simultaneous fascination with and revulsion from female sexuality, and a mingling of images of nineties' decadence with the petulance of a failed lover. Three poems are especially relevant here: the series of verses titled "Intrigue" from the *War Is Kind* volume, the poem from the same collection that begins "On the desert," and the updated brief verse, "A naked woman and a dead dwarf." "Intrigue" provides the most direct illustration of . . . transference of blame: the handwringing anguish and the accusations of infidelity swirl and spit out among verses of sentimental exaggeration.

> Thou art my love
> And thou art a weary violet
> Drooping from sun-caresses.
> Answering mine carelessly
> Woe is me.
> · · · · · ·
> Thou art my love
> And thou art the ashes of other men's love
> And I bury my face in these ashes
> And I love them
> Woe is me.
> · · · · · ·
> Thou art my love
> And thou art a priestess
> And in thy hand is a bloody dagger
> And my doom comes to me surely
> Woe is me.

The images are self-absorbed and angry. They sink to

bathos—"I weep and I gnash / And I love the little shoe / The little, little shoe"—and seldom rise beyond self-pity. The theme is struck here, as it will be frequently throughout Crane's work: women, being incapable of fidelity, make men into fools. Being without honesty, they make mockery of men's attempts to transcend human limits. Like the "little man" who inhabits so much of Crane's fiction, the lover is reduced to posturing and pomposity:

> God give me loud honors
> That I may strut before you, sweetheart
> And be worthy of—
> —The love I bear you
>
> to fantasies of brutality:
> And I wish to be an ogre
> And hale and haul my beloved to a castle
> And there use the happy cruel one cruelly
> And make her mourn with my mourning
>
> and of chivalry
>
> I have heard your quick breaths
> And seen your arms writhe toward me;
> At those times
> —God help us—
> I was impelled to be a grand knight.

But that, too, leads to self-mockery: the knight would "Swagger and snap my fingers, / And explain my mind finely."

The woman here, as in "On the desert," is like a snake: her arms "writhe" toward her lover. The echo of the Garden of Eden, the tempting snake, is combined with the popular nineties image of the sinuous Salomé in the shorter poem. . . .

WOMEN MAKE FOOLS OF MEN

The risk of being made a fool of, of being false to oneself, dominates Crane's view of men's fate in the presence of women. In "A naked woman and a dead dwarf" he strips both parties to the essentials. The man is the fool in cap and bells, truly the little man, the dwarf—and perhaps a more exact figure of impotence—and the woman is naked.

> A naked woman and a dead dwarf;
> Wealth and indifference.
> Poor dwarf!
> Reigning with foolish kings
> And dying mid bells and wine
> Ending with a desperate and comic palaver
> While before thee and after thee
> Endures the eternal clown—

—The eternal clown—
A naked woman.

Here the little man is clearly identified with the artist. "Ending with a desperate comic palaver," he endures the final humiliation. The woman survives.

The temptation to autobiographical readings of Crane's portraits of women is strong. But it is less fruitful to see this poem as simply Crane being angry in advance at his wife for outliving him than to see it within the context of the destructive tension between honesty and dishonesty, morality and immorality, the making of art and its destruction, that Crane sees as the relation between man and woman. In that relation, man and especially man as artist (there are no creative women in Crane) is driven into posturing and fantasy or forced into silence and self-betrayal.

The experiment in form that his poems represented apparently freed Crane to express the deeper associations of ideas and emotions that governed his imagination—bitterness, irony, and anger as well as a high romantic self- image are all more openly expressed. The fiction was a different matter: the stories were written to attract a large reading public and to earn him a living. There were forms ready to hand—the tract, the adventure story, the small-town tale—and he turned to them, while transforming each to suit his purposes. In so doing, Crane modified his portrayal of women but did not turn away from his conviction that they were the troublemakers, noisy, disloyal, and destructive.

Only passive women, those who could be rescued by men and be properly grateful for it, like Marjory Wainwright in *Active Service* (1899) or the bride who came to Yellow Sky, were exceptions. They allowed men to find and express their better selves: the married Jack Potter, Sheriff of Yellow Sky, defeats Scratchy Wilson once and for all, and without violence. His bride, "not pretty, nor . . . very young," the bearer of a "plain, under-class countenance," and rescued by Potter from the drudgery of being someone's cook, looks on. Rufus Coleman, the sophisticated, hard-drinking editor of the Sunday edition of the yellow *New York Eclipse,* rushes off to save Marjory and her parents from a terrible fate in the midst of the Greco-Turkish war. She, well trained in the modesty becoming a lady, maintains her dignity and transforms him into a figure of innocent happiness; *Active Service* ends in a romantic fade-out clearly designed to please the serial-reading audience for whom, in the rush of trying to finish the novel and pay his bills, Crane in the end designed the book. . . .

CRANE'S WIFE

The book's main interest is in the glimpses it gives of Crane's conception of the journalist's role. Many, however, have found extra interest in comparing Nora Black to Cora Stewart Crane, Crane's common-law wife. He had first met her in 1897 in Jacksonville, Florida, where he had gone preparatory to covering the insurrection in Cuba. Twice married and once divorced, Cora Stewart was the owner of the Hotel de Dream, a successful brothel. "The lady was handsome, of some real refinement, aloof to most," until she met Stephen Crane, with whom she fell deeply in love. He reciprocated. Older than he by some five or six years, eager—as her letters suggest—to care for him and yet tantalizingly unconventional, Cora Stewart had obvious attractions for the young writer who had put such energies into rebellion.

As her biographer suggests, Cora Stewart shared Crane's delight in defying the rules. "One of the greatest pleasures of having been what is called bad is that one has so much to say to the good. Good people love hearing about sin," she wrote. She had flaunted convention by walking out on her well-to-do English husband, Donald Stewart, when he refused her a divorce, and even more by making her way to Jacksonville and establishing her business there. She also shared Crane's romanticism, both its decadent side:

> Sometimes I like to sit at home and read good books, at others I must drink absinthe and hang the night hours with scarlet embroideries. I must have music and the sins that march to music

and its idealism:

> Love illuminated by truth, truth warmed through and through by love—these perform for us the most blessed thing that one human being can do for another.

Cora Stewart also wryly recognized certain "limits of decorum," both in romantic relationships and in business. "Zeus has unquestioned right to Io," she noted, "but woe betide Io when she suns her heart in the smiles that belong to Hera." She married her lovers, she was always seen in public with a woman companion, Mrs. Ruedy, and she promoted the Hotel de Dream as a place primarily for good food and good conversation. No hard liquor was served, and Cora Stewart maintained her dignity and her privacy, while charming men with her wit and conversation....

Hardest for Cora Crane must have been the realization that Stephen Crane was not content with their life. Early on, he had described to her his belief in the evanescence of love:

> Love comes like the tall swift shadow of a ship at night. There is for a moment, the music of the water's turmoil, a bell, perhaps, a man's shout, a row of gleaming yellow lights. Then the slow sinking of this mystic shape. Then silence and a bitter silence—the silence of the sea at night.

When war broke out in Cuba, Crane left England as fast as he could; he did not return for nine months, and his silence was indeed bitter to Cora. She had to abandon the dignity she so prized to write frantic letters to the United States seeking his whereabouts and to publishers seeking money to pay their bills. He returned to England and to her very slowly. Eighteen months later he was dead. Cora Crane returned to Jacksonville but her moment was past; she was never able to reestablish herself successfully in business, made a disastrous marriage, and died in her mid-forties in 1910....

DISHONESTY

Nora and the faithless lover of "Intrigue" share with the other women in Crane's poetry and fiction an inability to be honest—with themselves or, most important, with others. For Crane, honesty and its attendant virtue loyalty were the only means to redemption. In a much-quoted letter to John Hilliard, probably written in 1896, Crane spelled out his creed:

> I understand that a man is born into the world with his own pair of eyes, and he is not at all responsible for his vision—he is merely responsible for his quality of personal honesty. To keep close to this personal honesty is my supreme ambition. ...This aim in life struck me as being the only thing worth while. A man is sure to fail at it, but there is something in the failure.

Crane's formulation here parallels a distinction made earlier by his father, the Reverend Jonathan Townley Crane, regarding the relation between the neutral passions of human beings and their responsibility for self-control. In *Holiness, the Birthright of All God's Children* (1874), the elder Crane noted that "to be human is to be endowed with appetites and passions, innocent in themselves but unreasoning, required to be guided by the intellect and the conscience and controlled by the will." His example was Eve, who was to be condemned, not for her desire for the forbidden tree, but for her decision to yield. The premium put by both father and son on the exercise of choice and strength of will is reflected in Crane's assessment of his characters. Circumstances are no excuse, Crane often reiterated—the poor and the dependent have just as much chance to be virtuous. The daughters of Eve clearly have a harder time of it. Self-control, fidelity to a vision of personal honesty and responsibility are not among their gifts.

COMPARING CRANE'S WOMEN WITH MEN

Contrast, for example, groups of women and men. When men gather in Crane, they are seen to understand each other and to possess a comprehension of the large issues that precludes any unnecessary conversation. When women gather, it is to cackle and rant, to exult in disaster. When Maggie has been found drowned in the East River for her sins, her mother and her acquaintances convene:

> "Yer poor misguided chil' is gone now, Mary, an' let us hope it's fer deh bes'. Yeh'll fergive her now, Mary, won't yehs, dear, all her disobed'ence? All her tankless behavior to her mudder an' all her badness? She's gone where her ter'ble sins will be judged.". . . Two or three of the spectators were sniffling, and one was loudly weeping. . . . "She's gone where her sins will be judged," cried the other women, like a choir at a funeral.
> "Deh Lord gives and deh Lord takes away," responded the others.
> "Yeh'll fergive her, Mary!" pleaded the woman in black. The mourner . . . shook her great shoulders frantically, in an agony of grief. . . . Finally her voice came and arose like a scream of pain. "Oh, yes, I'll fergive her! I'll fergive her!"

. . . Compare the sound of these . . . women with Crane's account of men facing situations of moral and physical danger. Loyalty and brotherhood characterize the quiet communion of the men in "The Open Boat":

> The hurt captain, lying against the water-jar in the bow, spoke always in a low voice and calmly; but he could never command a more ready and swiftly obedient crew than the motley three of the dinghy. It was more than a mere recognition of what was best for the common safety. There was surely in it a quality that was personal and heartfelt. And after this devotion to the commander of the boat, there was this comradeship, that the correspondent, for instance, who had been taught to be cynical of men, knew even at the time was the best experience of his life. But no one said that it was

so. No one mentioned it.

The silence there is profound, even sacred; the men understand without speaking, as they do in the stress of battle in *The Red Badge of Courage* and others of the war stories. There are shrieks and cries there, but they are mechanical—the sounds of war machines—or the cry of pain and the shout of victory. While Maggie's death is celebrated by cannibalistic din, the death of Jim Conklin, through which Henry Fleming learns both the enormity of his sin and his path to redemption, is framed in silence:

> His spare figure was erect; his bloody hands were quietly at his side. He was waiting with patience for something that he had come to meet. He was at the rendezvous. They paused and stood, expectant.

There was silence.

Crane's two early fictions about women, *Maggie* and *George's Mother*, are loud with the sound of women, betraying their children and bemoaning their betrayal by them. *Maggie* was written when Crane was twenty-one; he published it himself a year later in 1893. He sent copies off to Hamlin Garland and to William Dean Howells, conscious that his small book was in the vein of realism that the older writers prized and hoping that his gesture of literary rebellion—as he saw it—would win him approval. The dedicatory note to Garland was repeated in other copies with only slight modification. Anticipating the reader's shock, he insisted that the book set out to show

> that environment is a tremendous thing... and frequently shapes lives regardless. If one proves that theory, one makes room in Heaven for all sorts of souls (notably an occasional street girl) who are not confidently expected to be there by many excellent people.

... *Maggie* is essentially a tract, written by the son of a gentle Methodist. Crane's father had left the Presbyterian church because he could not accept the doctrine of infant damnation. But he was nonetheless a stringent moralist....

By making Maggie so clearly working class, he ensured that her fall into prostitution and her suicide would not unduly disturb the reader. Indeed, the pattern of Maggie's fall might have come directly from the pages of the genteel reformers of the purity crusade. They saw that low wages and the resulting poor living conditions tempted young women to seek for something more. They warned, too, as had

Crane's father, against the dangers of alcohol and of popular entertainment, especially the melodramas of the kind to which Pete took Maggie. . . .

[Crane's] understanding of what led a girl into the life was exactly what one might expect from a well-brought-up young man. His behavior was rebellious: he associated with prostitutes and women of the demimonde as a way of proving his bohemianism, even though it brought personal risk. But when challenged, he responded out of his background. He defended the honor of Dora Clark, accused of soliciting, and appeared in police court on her behalf. The result was fierce attacks on him by the New York press and personal ostracism. He explained his claim to be married to a woman charged with soliciting: "If it were necessary to avow a marriage to save a girl who is not a prostitute from being arrested as a prostitute, it must be done though the man suffer eternal ruin."

Crane understood the language and the rules in a way that slum inhabitants could not; his rescue attempts could be successful, but Jimmie, Maggie's brother, could not perform the same service for her. He had "an idea that it wasn't common courtesy for a friend to come to one's house and ruin one's sister. But he was not sure how much Pete knew about the rules of politeness." Jimmie's sense of right and wrong is more than his mother or her friends possess, but the comment is nonetheless an easy joke at Jimmie's, and ultimately at Maggie's, expense.

In ascribing Maggie's downfall to what were a conventional set of causes—poverty, the harsh life of the shopgirl, the search for some excitement in a tedious and difficult life—Crane followed a pattern. He breaks it, however, by placing much of the blame for Maggie's fate on the women of the slums. Maggie herself becomes quickly and improbably accomplished in the ways of the streets, knowing to which men to appeal and which to avoid:

> A girl of the painted cohorts of the city went along the street. She threw changing glances at men who passed her, giving smiling invitations to men of rural or untaught pattern and usually seeming sedately unconscious of the men with a metropolitan seal upon their faces.

But Crane makes clear that she is neither successful nor willing at the game; her life as a prostitute is chiefly an occasion for hypocritical self-righteousness on the part of the other female inhabitants of the slums.

As an assault on Christian hypocrisy, Crane liked to recall the attacks on his mother by others when she took in a mother and her child born out of wedlock. Women are incapable, Crane clearly believed, of true charity ("Charity is a toy of women," one poem begins) and even of the kindness and loyalty that should go without saying for an innocent child, and particularly of a mother for her child. Mary Johnson, Maggie's mother, is a drunk, a grotesque, a figure of the angry and malevolent goddess of evil. Her tangled hair calls up the image of the snake, but her threat is not sexual. Her sexuality is only material for a police station joke: "'Mary, the records of this and other courts show that you are the mother of forty-two daughters who have been ruined. The case is unparalleled in the annals of this court.'" Mary Johnson devours her daughter in her dogged pursuit of her own survival, gorging on self-righteousness and feasting on the clichés of bourgeois morality to justify herself. Her neighbors eagerly join her ravening outbursts, outdoing one another in imaginary tales of Maggie's promiscuity and keening complacently over her death. . . .

"THE MONSTER"

The sexless, noisy, gossiping women return in "The Monster." Written in 1897 but not published until 1899, this story is a powerful blending of the sun-dappled fiction of the small town with an exploration of its potential for evil. Whilomville—a permutation of Port Jervis, New York, where Crane spent some happy years—was the setting for many of his most whimsical stories: "The Angel Child," "His New Mittens," and others appearing later under the title of *Whilomville Stories* (1900). Most have an edge to them, an awareness of the social hypocrisy in the town, but only in "The Monster" did he use the town as a setting for a morality play. The story turns on a complex moral problem, the question of Dr. Trescott's responsibility to his black serving man, Henry Johnson, who had saved the life of Trescott's son, Jimmie, in a fire. Henry became not only mad but a faceless monster. The question, as Trescott sees it, is one not of charity but of justice.

Henry Johnson is a grotesque of an archetypal kind, a figure at once human and nonhuman. Before the fire, the town could classify Henry with the other blacks in the town and thus dismiss him. Now, faceless, he is suddenly the unknowable in their midst, and they react with anger and resentment. Henry cannot respond, so they direct their fury at Trescott, who refuses to allow Henry to disappear from their lives.

No Sentimental Glamour

Author William Dean Howells reviewed Maggie *in the* New York World *on July 26, 1896, when it first appeared.*

[*Maggie*] is the study of a situation merely: a poor, inadequate woman, of a commonplace religiosity, whose son goes to the bad. The wonder of it is the courage which deals with persons so absolutely average, and the art that graces them with the beauty of the author's compassion for everything that errs and suffers. Without this feeling the effects of his mastery would be impossible, and if it went further or put itself into the pitying phrases it would annul the effects. But it never does this; it is notable how in all respects the author keeps himself well in hand. He is quite honest with his reader. He never shows his characters or his situations in any sort of sentimental glamour; if you will be moved by the sadness of common fates you will feel his intention, but he does not flatter his portraits of people or conditions to take your fancy.

The social life of Whilomville is run by strict if unspoken rules, with clear divisions between the men and the women. The men meet in Reifsnyder's barbershop where they discuss the issues involved in Trescott's determination to help Henry Johnson at whatever risk to himself. Although frightened, the men are at least aware of the importance and value of Trescott's decision; they can understand the abstract considerations that motivate him, although incapable of such courage themselves. The women, however, cannot even begin to understand. They gather in the backyards and kitchens only to gossip, telling tales of those frightened by Henry and whipping themselves into a frenzy of excitement over the affair.

> The overplus of information was choking Carrie. . . . "And, oh, little Sadie Winter is awful sick, . . . And poor old Mrs. Farragut sprained her ankle in trying to climb a fence. And there's a crowd around the jail all the time . . ."
>
> Kate heard the excited newcomer, and drifted down from the novel in her room. . . . "Serves him right if he was to lose all his patients," she said suddenly, in blood-thirsty tones. She snipped her words out as if her lips were scissors.

The men of Whilomville are doubly impotent, before their own inarticulateness and moral inadequacy in the face of Trescott's virtue, and before the simplistic fury of the women. Like the squat and dumb men on the desert, they are made fools of by the women. They take refuge in blaming them. Asking Trescott to send Henry away, the men chorus to each point in their argument, "It's the women."

Like Mary Johnson and the raucous women of the slums, if less coarse, the women of Whilomville are morally and socially deformed. Cannibalistic in their devouring of reputations, they are capable of common action only to destroy. As in *Maggie*, their chief victim is another woman, Grace Trescott, the doctor's wife, who sits alone, bereft and foolish amid her unused teacups as the story ends.

Chief among the women is the "old maid" figure of Martha Goodwin. In several ways, Martha Goodwin resembles the "feminine mule" of Port Jervis whom Crane described in an 1894 letter. That woman had "no more brains than a pig," but whenever "she grunts something dies howling. It may be a girl's reputation or a political party or the Baptist Church but it stops in its tracks and dies." Crane's longtime animus against this woman seems, both in his letter and in his later fictional reincarnations of her, in excess of the cause. He had taken a fifteen-year-old girl out for a buggy ride on Sunday: "Monday the mule addresses me in front of the barber's and says 'You was drivin' Frances out y'day' and grunted. At once all present knew that Frances and I should be hanged on twin gallows for red sins." The "big joke" in all this, Crane gleefully goes on, is that

> this lady in her righteousness is just the grave of a stale lust and every boy in town knows it. She occurred ruin at the hands of a farmer when we were all 10 or 11. But she is a nice woman and all her views of all things belong on the table of Moses.

Crane's own self-righteousness, and his pleasure in rehearsing the adolescent snicker over the woman's fate, suggest this attack as a mirror image of the attitude toward women's sexuality seen in the poems. He used this episode with little modification in his early romantic novel, *The Third Violet*, and his obsession with women's past loves has been noted in "Intrigue" and *Active Service*. In "The Monster," he draws again on the episode and the image to create the contradictory figure of Martha Goodwin. Like the feminine mule, Martha has opinions on every large issue and "argued constantly for a creed of illimitable ferocity." She emphasized her opinions with a sniff, which her antagonists received "like a bang over the head, and none was known to recover." She is also and "simply the mausoleum of a dead passion." Her fiancé had died young of smallpox, "which he had not caught from her," and she lives on in the house of her sister and brother-in-law. She is their victim: while her sister Kate is upstairs with her novel, Martha does nearly all the housework "in return for the privilege of existence." Desexed, she can stir up the ashes of passion only in the denunciation of others. But while the women tremble before her savage attacks, they are in "secret revolt" against her. Vulnerable in her dependency, sexless, and without a male defender, "she remained a weak, innocent, and pig-headed creature, who alone would defy the universe if she thought the universe merited the proceeding.". . .

DISLOYALTY

Maggie and "The Monster" are the most vivid illustrations of Crane's conviction of women's incapacity for loyalty, indeed, for moral abstractions of any kind. It is in their disloyalty to each other that women are inferior to men and unredeemable. Not for them the "subtle brotherhood" that allows men to save themselves through mutual self-sacrifice, nor the moment of self-discovery that enables them to transcend past mistakes, as Henry Fleming does, and go on toward redemption. When Maggie reaches the point of self-discovery, it is too late to do anything but, conventionally, to throw herself in the East River. The other women do not reach such a moment.

Crane's happiest letters are to his old schoolmates at Claverack. That boarding school experience seems to have established for him an ideal of companionship and loyalty, a team spirit, that no relationship with a woman or among women could ever match. And, it seems, his view of women never matured far beyond that level of experience. For most of his brief career, the solution was to remove himself, as artist and as man, to the battlefield and the decks of ships, to places where women could not follow.

CHAPTER 2

The Red Badge of Courage

The Red Badge of Courage Is America's First Modern Novel

John Berryman

Humanities professor John Berryman remains a well-known poet and the author of a biography of Stephen Crane. In the following article, Berryman contends that *The Red Badge of Courage* bridges the gap between Russian naturalist writer Leo Tolstoy and Ernest Hemingway. He believes that Crane's perspective on the individual and society is uniquely modern.

It is hard to see how anyone, except a casual reader, could overrate *The Red Badge of Courage* for patriotic reasons, because, though the book does indeed handle parts of the battle of Chancellorsville, it is not really about the Civil War. For instance, it shows no interest in the causes, meaning, or outcome of the war; no interest in politics; no interest in tactics or strategy. In this book, these failures are a merit. . . . Here we have only parts of one minor battle, seen from one ignorant point of view, that of a new volunteer. One would never guess that what has been called the first modern war was being studied. All the same, as from the weird diagrams of Samuel Beckett emerges the helpless horror of modern man, we learn, as we learn from few books, about the waiting, the incomprehension, rumor, frustration, anxiety, fatigue, panic, hatred not only of the enemy but of officers; about complaints of "bad luck" and the sense of betrayal by commanders. This is a losing army. Since every intelligent man has to be at some point afraid of proving himself a coward—which is what the ordeal of Crane's protagonist is about—the story presents itself to us initially as making some claim to universality. . . .

Excerpts from the chapter on Stephen Crane by John Berryman, in *The American Novel*, edited by Wallace Stegner. Copyright ©1965 by Basic Books, Inc. Reprinted by permission of BasicBooks, a division of HarperCollins Publishers, Inc.

CRANE'S IRONY

The scene of this extremely simple novel is laid in a single mind. It starts with soldiers speculating loudly about whether there is going to be a fight or not. Then "a youthful private" goes off to his hut: "He wished to be alone with some new thoughts that had lately come to him." This has the effect of understatement, putting so flatly the youth's debate with himself about his honor, but it is literal, besides introducing the theme of intense isolation that dominated Crane's work until a later story, his masterpiece, "The Open Boat," where human cooperation in face of the indifference of nature is the slowly arrived-at subject. In *Red Badge* his youth broods in private, having crawled into his dilemma, or hut, "through an intricate hole that served it as a door"—and the rest of the book provides a workout of the plight. On the first day he does well, and then runs away. A Union soldier clubs him in the panic retreat; Crane's ironic title refers to the "badge" of that wound; the youth is taken for a good soldier. He witnesses the death of his boyhood friend, the tall soldier, a true hero. Returned, by the kindness of a stranger, to his regiment, he is cared for as a combatant by the loud youth, toward whom he is also enabled to feel superior in that, scared earlier, Wilson entrusted him with letters to be sent in the event of his death and has now, shamefacedly, to ask for their return. Next day he fights like a hero or demon. Such is the story. Perhaps many readers take it as a novel of development, a sort of success story, and this view is encouraged by the climactic passage:

> He felt a quiet manhood, non-assertive but of sturdy and strong blood. . . . He had been to touch the great death, and found that, after all, it was but the great death. He was a man. . . .

It is possible to feel very uncomfortable with this way of looking at the book. For one thing, pervasive irony is directed toward the youth—his self-importance, his self-pity, his self-loving war rage. For another, we have only one final semiself-reproach for his cowardice and imposture:

> He saw that he was good. . . . Nevertheless, the ghost of his flight from the first engagement appeared to him and danced. There were small shoutings in his brain about these matters. For a moment he blushed, and the light of his soul flickered with shame.

I find it hard to believe that in this passage Crane is exonerating his hero without irony. Finally, we have very early in the book an indication of his pomposity (his mother's "I know how you are, Henry"), and there is pomposity in his final opinion of himself as a war demon. That would suggest a circular action, in the coward middle of which he appeared to reveal his real nature, or in fact did reveal it, by running. The irony embraces, then, all but the central failure.

It is easy to feel uncomfortable with this view, too—more particularly because the apparent wound of the first day is indeed a real wound, and its silent pretension is later justified. On the other hand, the irony never ends. I do not know what Crane intended. Probably he intended to have his cake and eat it too—irony to the end, but heroism too. Fair enough. How far did he fail?

Again I invoke, as praiseworthy, that which is not done. The youth is frantically afraid of being found out (he never is found out) but except in the passage just quoted he never suffers the remorse one would expect. Intimate as Crane is with his hero psychologically, still the view he takes of him is cold, unsentimental, remote. This certainly preserves him from any full failure (though there have been many reliable readers from the day the book was published to now who have not liked it, because they regarded it as artificial and sensational).

CRANE EXCLUDES HIS USUAL THEMES

The coldness leads to a certain impersonality, and it is a striking fact that some of Crane's deepest private interests find no place in the novel; in fact, they are deliberately excluded. Three of them are worth singling out. In his earlier novel, or long story, called *Maggie*, laid in New York's Bowery, Crane dramatized a distinct social philosophy—environmentalist, deterministic, and convinced that "the root of slum-life" was "a sort of cowardice." Yet his indifference to society in *The Red Badge* is complete, and it would not do to say "Of course it would be," for an army *is* society.

So with the matter of personal philosophy. We happen to know Crane's views perfectly, because he put them at length in letters to a girl (Nellie Crouse) by whom he was fascinated in 1895–96. He wrote:

> For my own part, I am minded to die in my thirty-fifth year [he died at 28, in 1900]. I think that is all I care to stand. I don't like to make wise remarks on the aspects of life but I will say that it doesn't strike me as particularly worth the trouble. The

final wall of the wise man's thought however is Human Kindness of course.

Exceptionally for him, Crane capitalized the two words. Now it might have been supposed that, bringing his hero through to maturity in *The Red Badge*, he would have concentrated in this area. But no. It seems impossible not to conclude that the splendid burst of rhetoric with which the novel concludes is just that, *in part*—a burst of rhetoric—and that Crane retained many of his reservations about his hero. As the wisest of modern British novelists, E.M. Forster, once observed, novels almost never end well: character desires to keep on going, whereas remorseless plot requires it to end. I hardly remember a better instance. Yet the last page is confidently and brilliantly done:

> It rained. The procession of weary soldiers became a bedraggled train, despondent and muttering, marching with churning effort in a trough of liquid brown mud under a low, wretched sky. Yet the youth smiled, for he saw that the world was a world for him, though many discovered it to be made of oaths and walking-sticks. He had rid himself of the red sickness of battle.

But *then* comes a sentence in which I simply do not believe. "He turned now with a lover's thirst to images of tranquil skies, fresh meadows, cool brooks—an existence of soft and eternal peace." In short we are left after all with a *fool*, for Crane knew as well as the next man, and much better, that life consists of very little but struggle. . . . The shutting out of his hero from his personal thought redeems for me, on the whole, the end of the book. . . .

A MODERN AUTHOR

All the categorical terms that have been applied to Crane's art are slippery, but let me deny at once that he was a naturalist. The naturalists—Frank Norris, say, and Theodore Dreiser—are accumulative and ponderous. Crane's intense selectivity makes him almost utterly unlike them. Crane himself, when hardly more than a boy, allied his creed to the realism preached—in revolt against the slack, contrived, squeamish standards of popular American fiction in the nineties—by his first admirers, William Dean Howells, then the country's leading critic, and a younger writer, Hamlin Garland. But Crane's work does not resemble theirs, either, and he seems to have meant, in his alliance, only that art should be "sincere" (one of his favorite words) and truthful. Like many another young genius, he regarded most writers as frauds and liars, and in fact perhaps most writers *are* frauds and liars. But epithets so vague as "sincere" and "truthful" tell us very little. The best term is undoubtedly that of his close friend, the far greater novelist, Joseph Conrad (though whether a *better* writer it is probably too soon to say), who observed in a letter to a mutual friend that "He is *the* only impressionist, and *only* an impressionist.". . .

The use of irony enters so deeply into most of Crane's finest work . . . that the simple term "impressionist" will hardly do, and my uncertain feeling is that Crane is best thought of as a twentieth-century author. Authorities date modern American literature, some from *The Red Badge* in 1895, some from the re-issue in the following year of *Maggie*. This critique is not the place for an exposition of the nature of irony in relation to Crane, but perhaps something of that will emerge from a summary study of his style. By way, though, of winding up the impressionist reservations, let me reinforce Conrad's label with a quotation from Crane:

> I understand that a man is born into the world with his own pair of eyes and he is not at all responsible for his vision—he is merely responsible for his quality of personal honesty. To keep close to this personal honesty is my supreme ambition.

Ill, dying indeed, hard-pressed with guests and fame and need for money, working incessantly, he said to a journalist visitor during his last year of life: "I get a little tired of saying, 'Is this true?'" He was an impressionist: he dealt in the way things strike one, but also in the way things are.

This famous style is not easy to describe, combining as it does characteristics commonly antithetical. It is swift, no style in English more so improvisatorial, . . . but at the same time it goes in for ritual solemnity and can be highly poetic. For example, as an illustration of the speed of his style:

> For a moment he felt in the face of his great trial like a babe, and the flesh over his heart seemed very thin. He seized time to look about him calculatingly.

Here we are already into something like the poetic tone which is well illustrated in the opening sentence of the novel: "The cold passed reluctantly from the earth, and the retiring fogs revealed an army stretched out on the hills, resting." This is a high case of the animism already referred to. The color of the style is celebrated; maybe he got it from a theory of Goethe's, but the style is also plain, plain. Short as it is, it is also unusually iterative; modern and simple, brazen with medieval imagery; animistic, dehuman, and mechanistic; attentive—brilliantly—to sound:

> As he ran, he became aware that the forest had stopped its music, as if at last becoming capable of hearing the foreign sounds. The trees hushed and stood motionless. Everything seemed to be listening to the crackle and clatter and ear-shaking thunder. The chorus pealed over the still earth.

Adverbs are used like verbs, word order deformed: somebody leans on a bar and hears other men "terribly discuss a question that was not plain." But the surest attribute of this style is its reserve, as its most celebrated is its color. Crane guarantees nothing. "Doubtless" is a favorite word. The technique of refusal is brought so far forward that a casual "often" will defeat itself: "What hats and caps were left to them they often slung high in the air." Once more we hear a Shakespearean contempt, as in *Coriolanus.* In a paradoxical way, if he will not vouch for what he tells us, if he does not push us, trying to convince, we feel that he must have things up his sleeve which would persuade us if we only knew them. As for color: "A crimson roar came from the distance" is the mildest example I have been able to find. His employment of it here is not only not naturalistic (what roar was ever red?) but is solely affective, that is, emotional, like his metaphorical use, in the novel, of devils, ghouls, demons, and specters. Crane made use of a spectrum. A final item is his rueful humor: "He threw aside his mental pamphlets on the philosophy of the retreated and rules for the guidance of the damned.". . .

Crane makes a sort of little bridge between Tolstoy—supreme—supreme?—and our very good writer Hemingway. But these superior gentlemen are not competitors. One of the most cogent remarks ever made about the poet of the *Iliad* is that he shared with Tolstoy and with Shakespeare both a virile love of war and a virile horror of it. So in his degree did Crane, and before he had seen it.

The Red Badge of Courage: Crane's Realism Makes the Novel Great

Joseph Conrad

Polish-born author Joseph Conrad met Crane near the end of Crane's life and the two struck up a friendship that lasted for several years. In the following essay, Conrad analyzes *The Red Badge of Courage* and praises the novel for its realistic depiction of war. Conrad believes that Crane's cunning portrayal of the soldier Henry Fleming imitates all humanity's struggle to understand life. Several of Joseph Conrad's novels are considered classics, including *Heart of Darkness, Lord Jim,* and *The Nigger and the Narcissus.*

One of the most enduring memories of my literary life is the sensation produced by the appearance in 1895 of Crane's *Red Badge of Courage* in a small volume belonging to Mr. Heinemann's "Pioneer Series of Modern Fiction"—very modern fiction of that time, and upon the whole not devoid of merit. I have an idea the series was meant to give us shocks, and as far as my recollection goes there were, to use a term made familiar to all by another war, no "duds" in that small and lively bombardment. But Crane's work detonated on the mild din of that attack on our literary sensibilities with the impact and force of a twelve-inch shell charged with a very high explosive. Unexpected it fell amongst us; and its fall was followed by a great outcry.

Not of consternation, however. The energy of that projectile hurt nothing and no one (such was its good fortune), and delighted a good many. It delighted soldiers, men of letters, men in the street; it was welcomed by all lovers of personal

Reprinted from Joseph Conrad, "A Preface to Stephen Crane's *The Red Badge of Courage,*" in *Last Essays* by Joseph Conrad (London: J.M. Dent, 1926).

expression as a genuine revelation, satisfying the curiosity of a world in which war and love have been subjects of song and story ever since the beginning of articulate speech.

Here we had an artist, a man not of experience but a man inspired, a seer with a gift for rendering the significant on the surface of things and with an incomparable insight into primitive emotions, who, in order to give us the image of war, had looked profoundly into his own breast. We welcomed him. As if the whole vocabulary of praise had been blown up sky-high by this missile from across the Atlantic, a rain of words descended on our heads, words well or ill chosen, chunks of pedantic praise and warm appreciation, clever words, and words of real understanding, platitudes, and felicities of criticism, but all as sincere in their response as the striking piece of work which set so many critical pens scurrying over the paper.

A MASTERPIECE

One of the most interesting, if not the most valuable, of printed criticisms was perhaps that of Mr. George Wyndham, soldier, man of the world, and in a sense a man of letters. He went into the whole question of war literature, at any rate during the nineteenth century, evoking comparisons with the *Memoires* of General Marbot and the famous *Diary of a Cavalry Officer* as records of a personal experience. He rendered justice to the interest of what soldiers themselves could tell us, but confessed that to gratify the curiosity of the potential combatant who lurks in most men as to the picturesque aspects and emotional reactions of a battle we must go to the artist with his heaven-given faculty of words at the service of his divination as to what the truth of things is and must be. He comes to the conclusion that:

"Mr. Crane has contrived a masterpiece."

"Contrived"—that word of disparaging sound is the last word I would have used in connection with any piece of work by Stephen Crane, who in his art (as indeed in his private life) was the least "contriving" of men. But as to "masterpiece," there is no doubt that *The Red Badge of Courage* is that, if only because of the marvellous accord of the vivid impressionistic description of action on that woodland battlefield, and the imagined style of the analysis of the emotions in the inward moral struggle going on in the breast of one individual—the Young Soldier of the book, the protagonist of the monodrama presented to us in an effortless succession of graphic and coloured phrases.

FLEMING AS EVERYMAN

Stephen Crane places his Young Soldier in an untried regiment. And this is well contrived—if any contrivance there be in a spontaneous piece of work which seems to spurt and flow like a tapped stream from the depths of the writer's being. In order that the revelation should be complete, the Young Soldier has to be deprived of the moral support which he would have found in a tried body of men matured in achievement to the consciousness of its worth. His regiment had been tried by nothing but days of waiting for the order to move; so many days that it and the Youth within it have come to think of themselves as merely "a part of a vast blue demonstration." The army had been lying camped near a river, idle and fretting till the moment when Stephen Crane lays hold of it at dawn with masterly simplicity: "The cold passed reluctantly from the earth. . . ." These are the first words of the war book which was to give him his crumb of fame.

The whole of that opening paragraph is wonderful in the homely dignity of the indicated lines of the landscape, and the shivering awakening of the army at the break of the day before the battle. In the next, with a most effective change to racy colloquialism of narrative, the action which motivates, sustains and feeds the inner drama forming the subjects of the book, begins with the Tall Soldier going down to the river to wash his shirt. He returns waving his garment above his head. He had heard at fifth-hand from somebody that the army is going to move to-morrow. The only immediate effect of this piece of news is that a negro teamster, who had been dancing a jig on a wooden box in a ring of laughing soldiers, finds himself suddenly deserted. He sits down mournfully. For the rest, the Tall Soldier's excitement is met by blank disbelief, profane grumbling, an invincible incredulity. But the regiment is somehow sobered. One feels it, though no symptoms can be noticed. It does not know what a battle is; neither does the Young Soldier. He retires from the babbling throng into what seems a rather comfortable dug-out and lies down with his hands over his eyes to think. Thus the drama begins.

He perceives suddenly that he had looked upon wars as historical phenomenons of the past. He had never believed

in war in his own country. It had been a sort of play affair.
He had been drilled, inspected, marched for months, till he
has despaired "of ever seeing a Greek-like struggle. Such
were no more. Men were better or more timid. Secular and
religious education had effaced the throat-grappling instinct, or else firm finance held in check the passions."

Very modern this touch. We can remember thoughts like
these round about the year 1914. That Young Soldier is representative of mankind in more ways than one, and first of
all in his ignorance. His regiment had listened to the tales of
veterans, "tales of grey bewhiskered hordes chewing to-
bacco with unspeakable valour and sweeping along like the
Huns." Still, he cannot put his faith in veterans' tales. Re-
cruits were their prey. They talked of blood, fire, and sudden
death, but much of it might have been lies. They were in no-
wise to be trusted. And the question arises before him
whether he will or will not "run from a battle"? He does not
know. He cannot know. A little panic fear enters his mind.
He jumps up and asks himself aloud, "Good Lord! What's
the matter with me?" This is the first time his words are
quoted, on this day before the battle. He dreads not danger,
but fear itself. He stands before the unknown. He would like
to prove to himself by some reasoning process that he will
not "run from the battle." And in his unblooded regiment he
can find no help. He is alone with the problem of courage.

In this he stands for the symbol of all untried men.

CRANE'S IMAGINATION

Some critics have estimated him a morbid case. I cannot
agree to that. The abnormal cases are of the extremes; of
those who crumple up at the first sight of danger, and of
those of whom their fellows say, "He doesn't know what fear
is." Neither will I forget the rare favourites of the gods whose
fiery spirit is only soothed by the fury and clamour of a battle. Of such was General Picton of Peninsular fame. But the
lot of the mass of mankind is to know fear, the decent fear of
disgrace. Of such is the Young Soldier of *The Red Badge of
Courage.* He only seems exceptional because he has got in-
side of him Stephen Crane's imagination, and is presented to
us with the insight and the power of expression of an artist
whom a just and severe critic, on a review of all his work, has
called the foremost impressionist of his time, as Sterne was
the greatest impressionist, but in a different way, of his age.

This is a generalised, fundamental judgment. More superficially both Zola's *La Débâcle* and Tolstoi's *War and Peace* were mentioned by critics in connection with Crane's war book. But Zola's main concern was with the downfall of the imperial régime he fancied he was portraying; and in Tolstoi's book the subtle presentation of Rostov's squadron under fire for the first time is a mere episode lost in a mass of other matter, like a handful of pebbles in a heap of sand. I could not see the relevancy. Crane was concerned with elemental truth only; and in any case I think that as an artist he is non-comparable. He dealt with what is enduring, and was the most detached of men.

That is why his book is short. Not quite two hundred pages. Gems are small. This monodrama, which happy inspiration or unerring instinct has led him to put before us in narrative form, is contained between the opening words I have already quoted and a phrase on page 194 of the English edition, which runs: "He had been to touch the great death, and found that, after all, it was but the great death. He was a man."

On these words the action ends. We are only given one glimpse of the victorious army at dusk, under the falling rain, "a procession of weary soldiers become a bedraggled train, despondent and muttering, marching with churning effort in a trough of liquid brown mud under a low wretched sky . . . ," while the last ray of the sun falls on the river through a break in the leaden clouds.

This war book, so virile and so full of gentle sympathy, in which not a single declamatory sentiment defaces the genuine verbal felicity, welding analysis and description in a continuous fascination of individual style, had been hailed by the critics as the herald of a brilliant career. Crane himself very seldom alluded to it, and always with a wistful smile. Perhaps he was conscious that, like the mortally wounded Tall Soldier of his book who, snatching at the air, staggers out into a field to meet his appointed death on the first day of battle while the terrified Youth and the kind Tattered Soldier stand by silent, watching with awe "these ceremonies at the place of meeting"—it was his fate, too, to fall early in the fray.

The Red Badge of Courage Mocks the Greek Epic

Chester L. Wolford

Critic Chester L. Wolford is the author of *The Anger of Stephen Crane: Fiction and the Epic Tradition,* from which this article is excerpted. Wolford argues that *The Red Badge of Courage* uses the form of the Greek epic to contrast Henry Fleming and the classical epic hero. Henry continues to become involved in situations that are epic in scale, yet even when he thinks he has faced and discarded illusion, and acted heroically, he is deluding himself.

The Red Badge of Courage establishes Stephen Crane as a writer formally and solidly within the great tradition established and fostered by Homer, Virgil, Milton, and others. While including many of the trappings and conventions and much machinery of formal epic, *The Red Badge* also shares with the epic a more essential quality: the tradition of epic competition. . . .

A GROUP IDENTITY

Throughout the first half of *The Red Badge,* the competition between the individualism of Henry's *areté* and the collectivism of . . . "heroic martyrdom" swings between extremes. In his first engagement, Henry seems finally to give in to the standards of the group: "He suddenly lost concern for himself and forgot to look at a menacing fate. He became not a man but a member. He felt that something of which he was a part—a regiment, an army, a cause, or a country—was in crisis. He was welded into a common personality which was dominated by a single desire." Soon, the group becomes even more important to him than the causes: "He felt the subtle battle brotherhood more potent even than the cause for which they were fighting. It was a mysterious fraternity."

Much has been made of Henry's joining the subtle brotherhood, but few remember that when the enemy makes a second charge against the regiment, the mysterious fraternity dissolves under an individuality revived by Henry's sense of self-preservation. He turns tail and runs. Although Achilles has more grace and style, the effect is the same in either case: both Henry and Achilles desert their friends in the field. To say, as many do, that Henry should be damned for his desertion is to speak from an historically narrow perspective; from an Homeric standpoint, one cannot be so quick to judge. In fact, no moral judgments necessarily result from Henry's flight. If Henry can get away with it (he does), if no one finds out about it (no one does), and if later he can perform "great deeds" (he does), then that is all that matters. By the end of the sixth chapter, Henry's individualism, his Homeric sense, seems to have won a limited victory—victory because Henry has escaped being subsumed by the group, limited because his sense of shame dogs him throughout the novel. . . .

JIM CONKLIN

In this quarter of the novel, Henry enters the "forest chapel," sees Jim Conklin die in a Christ-like way, and is mentally and verbally assaulted by the "tattered man." Here, too, he receives his "red badge of courage."

It should not be surprising in light of the epic structure that this section of *The Red Badge* is filled with religious imagery. Much critical ink has been spilt in a controversy over whether or not Crane, given his naturalistic bent and nihilist vision, intends Jim Conklin, for example, to represent Christ, or the tattered man to represent the Christian-group ideal; many feel that Crane himself was confused about it and that the novel fails because he fails to resolve the problem. From the standpoint of examining the traditional epic qualities of the book, there is no problem. These chapters mark what ultimately becomes a failure of the Christian-group value system—with two thousand years of indoctrination behind it—to make Henry Fleming return to the fold. It is not Crane's intent to have the reader see things in a religious way, but to see Henry succumb to the pathetic fallacy of Christian-colored glasses. . . .

It is also clear that Henry sees Jim Conklin in a "religious half light." Critic Stallman's original reading of Conklin as Christ is fundamentally correct if one understands that it is Henry and not Crane who sees Conklin as Christ. Few figures in American literature have a better claim to the trappings of Christ's Passion than does Jim Conklin. His initials are J.C., he is wounded in the side, he dies on a hill, he is a "devotee of a mad religion," and his death stirs "thoughts of a solemn ceremony." Those who deny that Conklin is a Christ-figure usually do so by pointing out that Conklin is a loud, cracker-crunching, rumormonger. Such evidence is specious, since these qualities are part of Jim only before he became "not a man but a member" by staying on the line during the battle. Some also forget that Crane's intent is to show that Henry sees Conklin in this way, not that Conklin is that way.

One way to place the various episodes of the first half into a perspective of the moral and social competition between Christian-group values and the Homeric ideal of individualism (*areté*) may be to describe that epic competition as a representation of the psychology of Christian conversion from an egocentric individualism to an altruistic membership in the flock. The pattern is familiar; as a moral being, man in Christian process moves from the commission of sin to guilt, to alienation, to a desire for expiation, to confession, and finally to redemption. In the end, the process fails to redeem Henry for Christianity, but it does give him a rough time of it, and it organizes the epic competition and psychology of the novel's first half.

Three particular episodes are representative of this psychological movement. The episodes with Mrs. Fleming, Jim Conklin, and the tattered man each appear to bring Henry steadily closer to rejecting his Homeric individuality while ultimately functioning ironically to force his acceptance of *areté*. By the time he is hit on the head and receives his "red badge of courage," Henry has sloughed off the Christian-group concept of heroism. His red badge is, however, not ironical in that he receives it for an act of cowardice; rather it is an outward sign—what the Greeks called *geras*—of his accomplishment in rejecting two thousand years of social and religious indoctrination. An epic feat. . . .

It is important to emphasize the universal qualities of the novel in general and of Henry Fleming in particular. He is at once common and uncommon; he is Man rebelling against his Mother, Mankind (or at least the archetypal American in the archetypal American novel) attempting to slough off the Past. . . .

DESTROYING THE PAST

Crane is using the formal epic ironically to destroy the traditions of heroism, and epic competition is used because its very purpose is to disparage what the past has considered to be the highest expression of man's duty, courage.

The Jim Conklin episode carries Henry a step further in the process by adding to sin and guilt the anguish of alienation and the desire for expiation through good works. After deserting the regiment and wandering through the forest, Henry joins a band of wounded men moving toward the rear. These men have stood their ground—for God and country possibly, for the group certainly. Their wounds seem to symbolize their sacrifices and their devotion to duty. Seeing them in this way, Henry feels alienated: "At times he regarded the wounded soldiers in an envious way. . . . He wished that he, too, had a wound, a red badge of courage." Such a badge would grant to Henry membership and acceptance in the group, would assuage his guilt and close the gap between himself and the others caused by his alienation. Henry's anguish is now greater than during the earlier episode: "He felt his shame could be viewed. He was continually casting sidelong glances to see if the men were contemplating the letters of guilt he felt burned in his brow." At this stage Henry is Stephen Crane's Dimmesdale, and the only difference between the two is that Crane's character ultimately is able to "put the sin at a distance." Hawthorne's protagonist never can.

Feeling that he bears the Mark of the Beast, Henry is then confronted by Jim Conklin's wounds, and in his already anguished state, Henry is quite ready to see in Jim an exceptional Christian devotion to duty and sacrifice for the group. Jim's actions, however, deny Henry expiation and even serve further to heighten his anxiety. Henry's attempts to receive absolution are repulsed, for Jim only wants to be left alone to die: "The youth put forth anxious arms to assist him, but the tall soldier went firmly on as if propelled. . . . The youth had reached an anguish where the sobs scorched him. He strove to express his loyalty. . . . The youth wished his friend to lean upon him, but the other always shook his head and strangely

protested. 'No—no—no—leave me be—leave me be—'
... and all the youth's offers he brushed aside." Henry's view
of Jim as a Christ is Henry's alone. The youth's attempts to
assuage his guilt in a bath of atonement fail; although he
asks, he does not receive—Jim Conklin will have none of it.
All that remains is Henry's very real and painful desire for
redemption. Redemption itself is as far away as ever.

Henry's Christian-group consciousness is pushed to its
limits in the "tattered man" episode. There are two "sins"
here: one is Henry's refusal to confess his earlier desertion
of the regiment, and the other is his desertion of the tattered
man, an act which redoubles his guilt. When Henry meets
the tattered man, the latter repeatedly asks him, "Where yeh
hit?" This question, asked over and over again, causes Henry
to feel the "letters of guilt" burned, Dimmesdale-like, into
his forehead. Instead of causing Henry to repent, however,
the letters merely force him to desert the wounded tattered
man and leave him to wander off into the fields to die. Immediately after deserting the tattered man, Henry's guilt
reaches almost unbearable proportions: "The simple questions of the tattered man had been knife thrusts to him. They
asserted a society that probes pitilessly at secrets until all is
apparent. . . . He could not keep his crime concealed in his
bosom. . . . He admitted that he could not defend himself."
Believing that "he envied those men whose bodies lay
strewn" on the field, he explicitly wants to be redeemed: "A
moral vindication was regarded by the youth as a very important thing."

Confused, guilt-ridden, and afraid that the group may discover his "sin," Henry's mind goes through, as in the first
chapter, the same metronomic movement between the demands of the group and the desires of the individual, but
with more pain. . . .

A BLOW TO THE HEAD

Henry is "reborn" after being hit on the head in chapter 12.
The language of the episode is carefully, even poetically,
rendered to represent rebirth. After watching a group of re-
treating soldiers, Henry runs down from a rise, grabs one of
the soldiers, and is clouted for his trouble:

> [The other soldier] adroitly and fiercely swung his rifle. It
> crushed upon the youth's head. The man ran on.
> The youth's fingers had turned to paste upon the other's

arm. The energy was smitten from his muscles. He saw the flaming wings of lightning flash before his vision. There was a deafening rumble of thunder within his head.

Suddenly his legs seemed to die. He sank writhing to the ground. He tried to arise. In his efforts against the numbing pain he was like a man wrestling with a creature of the air.

There was a sinister struggle.

Sometimes he would achieve a position half erect, battle with the air for a moment, and then fall again, grabbing at the grass. His face was of a clammy pallor. Deep groans were wrenched from him.

At last, with a twisting movement, he got upon his hands and knees, and from thence, like a babe trying to walk to his feet. . . . he went lurching over the grass.

He fought an intense battle with his body. His dulled senses wished him to swoon and he opposed them stubbornly, his mind portraying unknown dangers and mutilations if he should fall upon the field. He went tall soldier fashion.

Structurally, the passage focuses first on the falling away of the old in a metaphorical death. Henry loses his sight, his hearing, and then his ability to stand erect. In the middle is a five-word, one-sentence paragraph describing a "sinister struggle" between life and death. From there, the reborn Henry gets up on his hands and knees "like a babe," and finally is able to walk. In spite of the almost allegorical nature of the passage, its essence remains one of a very physical, almost literal, and, most important, quite individual rebirth.

One cannot help but think that the anthropological cast of the passage is intentional. At least, it demonstrates that Crane, however unconsciously, was aware of the consequences for thought of the Darwinian revolution. For Henry, as for mankind, the traditional past could no longer provide solace. Indeed, as the second half of *The Red Badge* shows, the traditional past had to be rolled up and replaced by naturalism and impressionism. . . .

Henry's wandering off "tall soldier fashion" after receiving the blow on the head does not mean that Henry has been converted to a group view of things. To see Jim as a Christian-group figure is to make the same mistake Henry made. Strip away the dramatic symbolism of Henry's former vision of Conklin and one is left with a man dying, alone, unwilling to be helped, and as afraid of mutilation as any Homeric hero. Speech and action are "real"; Henry's interpretation of them may not be. When Henry thus goes "tall soldier fashion," it is not necessarily as a Christ-figure. Henry is in no shape at this point to interpret events; in this instance, the information comes directly from the narrator. The dying Jim Conklin and the wounded Henry Fleming are linked, or seem to be linked, only by a desire to escape the group.

Wandering in the gathering darkness, Henry is finally given direction by an epic guide. Like the role of the captain in "The Reluctant Voyagers," the function of the "cheery man" is traditional to the machinery of epic. As Ariadne helps Theseus, Thetis comforts Achilles, Athena aids Odysseus, Venus supports and guides Aeneas, and Virgil leads Dante, so the cheery man helps Henry to gain self-control, and, as Gibson points out, places him in a position to confront those forces which he otherwise would have little power to oppose but which he must overcome in order to complete his epic task. The cheery man leads Henry back to the regiment.

. . . Henry appreciates, albeit somewhat after the fact, the cheery man's help. And well he should, for as he staggers towards the campfires of his regiment in the beginning of the second half of *The Red Badge*, he has nearly done the impossible. In a sense, he has performed more courageously than Achilles. Peliades had only to reach his goal of *areté*, while Fleming had first to throw off his sense of sin and alienation. On one level, he has suffered all the slings and "arrows of scorn" that can be shot at an individual by the archers of conscience, guilt, and alienation from the group. On another level, Henry has forced his way back through two millennia of nationalism and Christianity. Such an act is impossible for an ordinary man. To oppose and overcome, even to a limited degree, the teachings of secular and religious culture is an almost incredible, even epic, feat. . . .

VICTORIES

The epic tradition demands that a writer replace former concepts of epic heroism with his own if he wishes to be more than a mere imitator. In nearly all of Crane's best work, his idea of heroism is his ideal of personal honesty. Repeatedly, Crane measures his characters against this standard; Henry Fleming measures as well as any.

More than any other sort of writer, one whose work has epic dimensions lends to his fictional heroes his own supreme ambition; so much is this so, in fact, that the poet himself may be considered the ultimate hero of his own epic, and is sometimes difficult to separate from the fictional hero. For millennia the epic poet has been set apart from his fellows by his abilities, but especially by the intensity of his vision and by the degree to which he believes in it. For Crane, keeping close to his vision, in terms both of apprehension and of comprehension, is the standard not only of honesty but of heroism as well.

The desire to see clearly runs through *The Red Badge of Courage*. Henry in particular seeks continually to perceive with his own eyes. There are more than two hundred references in *The Red Badge* to Henry seeing, not seeing, or trying to see. However, his sight tends always to be obscured either by the group, which limits what the individual can see, or by a kind of Homeric hero complex in which Henry feels that an individual can see everything. Each is a form of blindness and each corresponds to one of the two epic value systems. There is an implication throughout most of the novel (the implication becomes explicit in the last chapter) that history is little more than an individual interpretation of events raised to a level of cultural reporting and collective interpreting. Both as individual and as representative man, Henry makes his own specific interpretations of events. On the other hand, those interpretations are also colored by epic concepts. If the individual's interpretation is deluded, so is the epic's, and vice-versa.

Since Crane uses "vision" as a metaphor for his own particular notion of heroism, former notions of epic heroism are first debased and then replaced by the use of images and references to seeing. One of the value systems attacked in *The Red Badge* is the Christian-group view, which obscures and distorts the attempts of the individual to "see." The group, in the form of the army or the brigade or the regiment, is constantly associated with smoke or fog. As Henry is about to move into his first engagement, he identifies the fog with the army; indeed, the fog seems to emanate from the group: "The youth thought the damp fog of early morning moved from the rush of a great body of troops." The same image is used in the opening sentence of the novel: "The cold passed reluctantly from the earth, and the retiring fogs revealed an army stretched out on the hills, resting.". . .

The group is also seen in terms of darkness, snakes, and monsters, which in epics and archetypes of the unconscious are usually identified with evil. As the army is forming to march into battle, Henry perceives the group: "From off in the darkness, came the trampling of feet. The youth could

occasionally see dark shadows that moved like monsters."
As the "monsters" moved off in columns, "there was an occasional flash and glimmer of steel from the backs of all
these huge crawling reptiles." And the "two long, thin, black
columns" appear "like two serpents crawling from the cav-
ern of the night." The men of the group themselves sometimes appear "satanic" to Henry. . . .

A Changing Vision of the Self

If the group influence which Henry has resisted and over
which he has gained some dominance causes the individual
to see less than he is able, the Homeric view of man purports
to allow the individual to "see" more than he actually can.
Crane renders the Homeric view meaningless by showing
that it too is clouded. . . . Henry, the Homeric hero, becomes
so caught up in his individual desires that his eyes are reduced to "a glazed vacancy." He becomes a "barbarian, a
beast." He sees himself as a "pagan who defends his religion," and he sees his battle-rage as "fine, wild, and, in some
ways, easy. He had been a tremendous figure, no doubt. By
this struggle he had overcome obstacles which he had admitted to be mountains. They had fallen like paper peaks,
and he was now what he called a hero."

The whole of chapter 17 describes Henry as being in the
grip of the blind battle-rage of Homeric heroes. He forgets
that he is merely a private engaged in a small charge on one
day of one battle. He thinks of himself as colossal in size and
of the other soldiers as "flies sucking insolently at his
blood." Although his neck is "bronzed" and he fires his rifle
with a fierce grunt as if he were "dealing a blow of the fist
with all his strength," he is essentially what one soldier calls
this "war devil": "Yeh infernal fool." Heroic Henry certainly
is, even in a traditional way, but a bit foolish as well.

Henry soon gains a truer vision. Going . . . to get some
water, Henry, as well as his image of himself as a Homeric
hero, is deflated by a "jangling general" who refers to Henry's
regiment, and implicitly to Henry himself, as a lot of "mule
drivers." Henry, who had earlier viewed nature as a sympa-
thetic goddess in language filled with Virgilian pathetic fallacy and Christian symbolism (the forest-chapel, for example), and later as a capricious, sometimes malevolent beast
much as Homer saw it, now has "new eyes" and sees himself
as "very insignificant." This is not necessarily a Christian

sense of insignificance, nor even a completely naturalistic one, but simply a realization that compared with more powerful forces, including the regiment, he is powerless. Moreover, since officers are often associated with gods, the sun, and other natural and supernatural entities, Henry's discovery can be seen as developing from his earlier views of nature.

After discovering his insignificance, Henry is in a position to receive a new heroism, a new vision, a "real" vision. In his charge across the field on the second day of battle, it "seemed to the youth that he saw everything":

> Each blade of the green grass was bold and clear. He thought that he was aware of every change in the thin, transparent vapor that floated idly in sheets. The brown or gray trunks of the trees showed each roughness of their surfaces. And the men of the regiment, with their starting eyes and sweating faces, running madly, or falling, as if thrown headlong, to queer, heaped up corpses—all were comprehended. His mind took a mechanical but firm impression, so that afterward everything was pictured and explained to him, save why he himself was there.

A "mechanical" impression of some blades of grass, tree trunks, and sweating, frightened, dying men: that is all one can ever hope to see. The process of epic has been reversed. Virgil had expanded Homer's view of ten or twenty years of glory on the plains before a small town in Asia Minor to include a long-lived empire encompassing the known world. Similarly, the Christian epics of Charlemagne and the crusades are described as world wars. Milton extended the epic beyond human time and farther out than human space. Crane doubled back upon the epic tradition, gradually narrowing space until the epic vision includes only a minute perception and compressing time until that perception exists only for a fleeting instant. It is epical in its achievement and heroic only because Crane has shown it to be the only vision possible for man that remains "bold and clear."

Tiny but unobscured by the smoke of the group . . . Henry's vision has made him Crane's version of the best epic hero. Trying to "observe everything" in his first battle, but failing to "avoid trees and branches," Henry now sees only *something*. Gone is the Roman vision of national destiny and the Miltonic perception of a Puritan God's universe. Heroism is defined in *The Red Badge* as one man's limited but perhaps illusionless vision: grass blades, tree trunks, dying men. . . .

THE LAST CHAPTER

The last chapter is an ironic recapitulation of each epic value system present in the remainder of the book. Homeric *areté* is savagely mocked, as is Christian-group heroism. The primary target, however, is that final concept of heroism, Crane's own, which Henry has achieved earlier: that concept based only on the individual's ability to peer into the pit of reality with a gaze unclouded by cultural and epic notions of what the world is like. Throughout this final chapter, Henry's (and Crane's) perception-based, impressionistic heroism is mocked by means of an ironic significance attached to images of and references to the sense of sight. Henry enters the chapter a cleareyed hero; he exits blind and deluded.

As the chapter opens, the battle has begun to wane and the sounds of war have begun "to grow intermittent and weaker." Henry's newfound vision soon runs the gamut of perception from egotistical pride to cringing guilt and humility, and is, in effect, also becoming "weaker." As the regiment begins to "retrace its way" like a snake "winding off in the direction of the river," Henry is with it, recrossing the Stygian stream he had crossed in chapter 3. Similarly, Henry's mind is "undergoing a subtle change": "It took moments for it to cast off its battleful ways and resume its accustomed course of thought. Gradually his brain emerged from the clogged clouds and at last he was enabled to more closely comprehend himself and his circumstance." After "his first thoughts were given to rejoicings" because he had "escaped" the battle, Henry's vision becomes distorted. First, he contemplates his "achievements." With Homeric eyes he sees his deeds as "great and shining." His deluded vision is so distorted that he dresses those deeds in the royal "wide purple and gold," which, on Henry, give off sparkles "of various deflections."

Next, he assumes Christian eyes, and his visions of Homeric glory, of *areté*, are destroyed by an exaggerated guilt brought on by the memory of his crime against the tattered man. The tattered man had tormented him unmercifully, but all Henry sees is a grotesquely distorted image of the gentle tattered man transmogrified into a weird Christian version of some apostle of revenge who visits on Henry a "vision of cruelty." One delusion displaces another, so that Henry's previous vision, as well as his heroism, becomes changed and meaningless, because no longer is it his alone. Homeric pride makes Henry a strutting fool, and Christian-group guilt betrays him as a coward. . . .

Henry's progression toward heroism during the first twenty-three chapters reverses and inverts itself in the last chapter, for Henry's vision is a distortion that destroys his notion of Homeric bravery and of *areté*. Henry's semi-sin of leaving the tattered man haunts him. . . . After recognizing that he had sinned, Henry receives partial expiation in the form of partial forgetfulness: "Yet he gradually mustered force to put the sin at a distance. And at last his eyes seemed to open to some new ways. He found that he could now look back upon the brass and bombast of his earlier gospels and see them truly. He was gleeful when he discovered that he now despised them." Henry here exchanges one false view of himself for another. The Homeric vision has given way to a Christian-group one. Crane, with beautiful, lyric irony, moves Henry away from the war and from the battle in his mind: "So it came to pass that as he trudged from the place of blood and wrath his soul changed." Henry now believes that "the world was a world for him," as a Christian-group hero should.

There is yet another way, however, in which Crane sets about to destroy the epic. By ironically disparaging the epic view of man's history, Crane ridicules the concept that readers have of the epic genre. The epic has long been one of the more revered forms of historical interpretation and cultural expression. Through epic poetry Homer presents man as a godlike animal struggling to gain a measure of immortality through the public recognition of great deeds. But the Homeric man was like Lear in the storm—alone, naked, and "unaccommodated"—and this is probably why Crane preferred this view more than other traditional views. . . . Virgil gave man more hope by giving him the opportunity to identify and merge with the immortality of a national group. By interpreting history in terms of a great empire, he was also in some measure espousing a kind of immortality. Medieval and Renaissance epic, including *The Song of Roland* and Tasso's *Gerusalemme liberata*, glorified the church militant, ordained to victory. Milton went even farther. He regarded man as completely unworthy of immortality, but acknowledged man's hope in a merciful God's love; man's earthly history spans the interval between creation and final redemption.

Crane felt that these interpretations of history were, to one degree or another, part of a giant hoax willfully perpetrated on man by man. At times he could be downright Aeschylean: "Hope," as Berryman quotes him, "is the most vacuous emotion of mankind."

The Red Badge is a denial of the epic view of history, which Crane felt creates an absurd, illusory, and vacuous emotion. . . .

In the last chapter, history becomes what memory becomes—a mechanism for man to build his self-image. Through the two main thrusts of the history of Western civilization, as expressed by the epic genre, man is deluded into believing himself to be either more or less than he actually is. In the end, Henry is led by his memory to believe with conviction all the mad, distorted hopes of epic history. Ironically, "at last his eyes opened on some new ways." These are new ways only for Henry; they are as old as history. . . .

The final delusion of history and memory Crane repudiated is that of "hope." Part of the reason that Virgil and Milton wrote epics was to give men hope. Beautifully parodic, and powerfully ironic, the last paragraphs of *The Red Badge* express the hopes of Aeneas and Adam, of Columbus and Hiawatha, and of people at all times and in all places, hot to cool, hard to soft, pain to pleasure, hell to heaven:

> So it came to pass that as he trudged from the place of blood and wrath, his soul changed. He had come from hot-ploughshares to prospects of clover tranquility and it was as if hot-ploughshares were not. Scars faded as flowers.

> It rained. The procession of weary soldiers became a bedraggled train, despondent and muttering, marching with churning effort, in a trough of liquid brown mud under a low, wretched sky. Yet the youth smiled, for he saw that the world was a world for him though many discovered it to be made of oaths and walking-sticks. . . . The sultry nightmare was in the past. He had been an animal blistered and sweating in the heat and pain of war. He turned now with a lover's thirst, to images of tranquil skies, fresh meadows, cool brooks; an existence of soft and eternal peace.

No one lives a life of "soft and eternal peace," except in deluded dreams, and Crane knew it. "He was almost illusionless," Berryman said of Crane, "whether about his subjects or himself. Perhaps his only illusion was the heroic one; and not even this . . . escaped his irony."

The Red Badge of Courage Redefined the War Novel

Amy Kaplan

Amy Kaplan is an assistant professor of English
and American studies at Mount Holyoke College.
In addition to studies of Stephen Crane, Kaplan has
written about William Dean Howells, Edith Wharton,
and American realism. In the following selection,
Kaplan argues that Crane is interested not in
historical veracity in *The Red Badge of Courage*,
but in reinterpreting the war, both culturally and
politically, for his nineteenth-century audience.

The year that saw the publication of *The Red Badge of
Courage* to great acclaim on both sides of the Atlantic was
reviewed as a time of "wars and bloodshed" by Joseph
Pulitzer's New York *World*. The newspaper's year-end survey
of 1895 recalled that "from Japan westward to Jackson's
Hole, bloodshed has encircled the globe," and it listed some
examples of contemporary wars:

> When the year 1895 dawned the Italians were engaged in a
> bloody war with the Abyssinians; Haiti was overrun by
> rebels, who had burned the capital, Port-au-Prince, and
> slaughtered many people; the French were preparing for
> their disastrous if victorious war in Madagascar; the Dutch
> were slaughtering the natives of Lombok, one of their depen-
> dencies in southeastern Asia; and rebellions were in progress
> in several of the South American countries.

To newspaper readers in 1895, these outbreaks of international violence may have seemed remote from America's geographical borders and even more distant in time from the
historic battlefields of America's last major conflict, the Civil
War. Yet as the decade progressed, the United States ven-
tured more boldly into international disputes; after verging

Reprinted from Amy Kaplan, "The Spectacle of War in Crane's Revision of History," in
New Essays on The Red Badge of Courage, edited by Lee Clark Mitchell. Copyright
©1986 by Cambridge University Press. Reprinted by permission of Cambridge University Press.

on military engagements with Italy, Chile, and Britain in the early 1890s, America fought a war against Spain in Cuba and the Philippines in 1898. Mass-circulation newspapers like the *World,* which had already made exotic battles in European colonies a staple for American consumption, had an enthusiastic audience feasting on the spectacle of the Spanish-American War. One year after covering the Greco-Turkish War, Stephen Crane landed in Cuba with the American marines as a special correspondent for Pulitzer. Datelined June 22, 1898, the *World* headline for the first major battle of the Spanish-American War read: "THE RED BADGE OF COURAGE WAS HIS WIG-WAG FLAG."

What do these international wars have to do with *The Red Badge of Courage,* a novel begun in 1893 about an internecine conflict that took place thirty years earlier? Although Crane himself had not yet seen a battle when he wrote his book, the heightened militarism in America and Europe at the end of the nineteenth century shapes his novel as much as does the historical memory of the Civil War. Crane's novel participates in a widespread cultural movement to reinterpret the war as the birth of a united nation assuming global power and to revalue the legitimacy of military activity in general. The novel looks back at the Civil War to map a new arena into which modern forms of warfare can be imaginatively projected.

This conjunction of past and present may help explain the paradoxical status that *The Red Badge of Courage* has long held as *the* classic American Civil War novel that says very little about that war. Crane divorces the Civil War from its historical context by conspicuously avoiding the political, military, and geographical coordinates of the 1860s, and he equally divorces the conflict from a traditional literary context by rejecting generic narrative conventions. The novel reduces both history and the historical novel to what its main character thinks of as "crimson blotches on the page of the past." The illegibility of history in Crane's war novel has informed most critical approaches, which either treat it as a statement about war in general, turn war into a metaphor for psychological or metaphysical conflicts, reconstruct the absent historical referents of the Civil War battlefield, or decry the weakness of the historical imagination in American literature. Contrary to these critical assumptions, Crane wrenches the war from its earlier contexts, not to banish history from his "Episode" but to reinterpret the war through the cultural lenses and political concerns of the late nineteenth century.

If, on the battlefield of *The Red Badge of Courage,* Crane does not revisit old territory with a historical imagination, he does explore an unfamiliar social landscape reminiscent of the modern cityscape of his earlier writing and replete with similar social tensions. Like other well-known novels of its time, Crane's is a book about social change, about the transition not only from internecine to international conflict or from preindustrial to mechanized forms of warfare, but also from traditional to modern modes of representation. The novel implicitly contributes to and criticizes the contemporary militarization of American culture by focusing not on politics but on the problem of representing war. Crane transforms the representation of war from a shared experience that can be narrated in written or oral stories into an exotic spectacle that must be viewed by a spectator and conveyed to an audience. This transformation was to provide Crane with a lens for reporting the real wars he observed in Greece and Cuba only two years after writing his Civil War novel. . . .

A TIMELESS LAND

Lacking the familiar signposts of historical and geographical names and dates, Crane's battlefield does indeed appear as a timeless new and unknown land, divorced from any particular social context. Yet Crane delineates a social dimension of his landscape, which both explains the appeal of the chivalric revival for the youth of the 1890s and circumscribes its limits. The social geography of *The Red Badge of Courage* resonates with the tensions of the late nineteenth century, a period in which warfare provided the most common vocabulary for the violent class conflicts that erupted in America's cities. From the Great Railroad Strike of 1877 to the Haymarket Riot of 1886 to the Pullman Strike of 1894, labor struggles pitted workers against local police and state militias and threatened to engulf the entire nation in an apocalyptic battle. Problems and solutions alike were articulated in martial language: In Edward Bellamy's popular novel of 1888, *Looking Backward,* the army provided the model for a peaceful industrial utopia, and in 1894 Coxey's "army" of the poor marched in protest on Washington. Some social critics, such as the missionary Josiah Strong, blamed the intensity of urban conflicts on the closing of the frontier and advocated United States expansion abroad, with its concomitant militarism, as the only relief for these domestic social conflicts.

A BOY'S DREAM OF WAR

There was no real literature of our Civil War, excepting the forgotten "Miss Ravenall's Conversion" by J.W. De Forest, until Stephen Crane wrote "The Red Badge of Courage.". . . Crane wrote it before he had ever seen any war. But he had read the contemporary accounts, had heard the old soldiers, they were not so old then, talk, and above all he had seen Mathew Brady's wonderful photographs. Creating his story out of this material he wrote that great boy's dream of war that was to be truer to how war is than any war the boy who wrote it would ever live to see. It is one of the finest books of our literature and . . . it is all as much of one piece as a great poem is.

Ernest Hemingway, introduction to *Men at War*, 1992.

Although it is a critical commonplace that Crane uses war as a metaphor for city life in his urban writing, it is less noted that he inverts this metaphor in *The Red Badge of Courage.* He describes the battlefield with urban metaphors that overlay the countryside and leave only traces of the rural landscape. The approaching army is described as a train, for example; soldiers become "mobs" and "crowds," and officers are compared to political bosses cajoling the masses. The battle itself is repeatedly called a vast "machine" that produces corpses and works according to mysterious orders. The main character moves from a farm into an army whose conditions resemble those of the industrial city of the late nineteenth century. There he finds not the chivalric adventures he sought but the anonymous and "monotonous life in a camp." He also finds a social structure that is ridden with class tensions between officers and privates. Indeed, the novel represents more verbal expressions of hostility and physical acts of violence between members of the Union army than against enemy troops, who remain invisible on the battlefield. We see an officer beating a frightened recruit, for example; a fellow soldier wounds Henry; and he engages in hand-to-hand combat only with the corpse of the Union color bearer who refuses to loosen his grip on the flag.

These social conditions of army life overwhelm Henry with a sense not simply of overcivilized ennui but, more importantly, of powerlessness. Outrage against his impotence provides his strongest motivation for acting, both when he runs away and when he fights, and it takes specific shape in his hatred of his superiors, a hatred that far outstrips any emotion directed toward the enemy. Henry's final feats of heroism are spurred by his resentment toward the conversation he overhears between two officers; expecting "some great, inner historical things," he and his friend instead listen to the officers refer to the troops as "mule-drivers." For Henry, this shockingly confirms his mother's prediction: "he was very insignificant. The officer spoke of the regiment as if he referred to a broom." The officers' conversation pierces Henry's chivalric sense of self with language that recalls those figures rejected by the narrator in the first chapter. Henry and his comrades replace the black teamster as the work horses of the industrial army, and their heroism is deflated by the domestic reference to brooms. Henry and his friend cannot directly express their "unspeakable indignation" at the officer, except by fighting even more viciously, to the point where they seem "like tortured savages."

Although Henry resents the machinery of war and the powerlessness it entails and envisions himself as a primitive warrior to escape from this machine, his atavistic fantasies, rather than offering him an escape, entrench him more solidly in the machinery of the army. In the midst of the fight, the officers he resents so vehemently become his comrades-in-arms, and they transcend internal friction in the heat of the battle. When the colonel praises the youth and his friend for their fervor, "they speedily forgot many things. The past held no error and disappointment. They were very happy and their hearts swelled with grateful affection for the colonel and the lieutenant." In 1894, a year of violent strikes in the midst of a major depression, the popular syndicated version of *The Red Badge of Courage* ended here, with the privates reconciled with their superiors. Although it would be simplistic to reduce the novel to a social allegory, the tensions between officers and privates, between social classes, are externalized and transcended on the battlefield, and the mob of soldiers is channeled into the machine. War is transformed from a means of expressing conflict to a way of purging internal social conflict, which was the argument set forth for overseas expansion in the 1890s.

In the longer version of the book published in 1895, Henry moves beyond this social reconciliation to the more abstract harmony between the individual and the machine: "he emerged from his struggles, with a large sympathy for the machinery of the universe." Once Henry has proven his manhood on the battlefield, the "gigantic machine" no longer serves as a metaphor for war. Instead, it becomes a symbol of a cosmic order that gently embraces the individual soldier. The martial ideal plays a mediating role in this reconciliation. Mechanical order and primitive abandon are interdependent discourses; Henry's stories of chivalric heroism both fuel and are swallowed up by the machinery of modern warfare. Thus, by fusing industrial and chivalric language, Crane exposes the function of the revival of the martial ideal and shows that it criticizes a rationalized and hierarchical social order only to reinforce it. . . .

FICTION IN WAR

Crane's revision of the history and story of the Civil War as a spectacle links his imaginative rendition of a war he never experienced to his later career as a foreign correspondent, covering the Greco-Turkish and Spanish-American wars in the late 1890s. Crane reportedly jumped at the chance to see a real war in order to prove that *The Red Badge of Courage* was "all right." Although he may have found that these wars verified his realism, his reports and fiction also show that the framework of the spectacle established in the novel provided a lens peculiarly suited to view international warfare in the 1890s.

"Jingoism is merely the lust of the spectator," wrote a British contemporary of Crane's, J.A. Hobson, in one of the first major studies of imperialism. Hobson compared the vicarious aggression of a spectator at a sporting event to the emotions of the jingoist, who remains "unpurged by any personal effort, risk or sacrifice, gloating over perils, pains and slaughter of fellow men who he does not know, but whose destruction he desires in a blind and artificially stimulated passion of hatred and revenge."[1] "The lust of the spectator" is both gratified and further aroused only in the act of watching, which distances the viewer while tantalizing him with the possibility of action. According to Hobson, who served as a journalist in the Boer War, the newspaper plays a crucial domestic role in arousing the spectatorial lust that supports imperial ventures in remote territories. Coinciding with the development of a mass circulation press in Britain and the United States, the international conflicts of the late nineteenth century created a new need for foreign correspondents to bring home the meaning of wars that "did not directly concern the future of the two countries where the major reading-public resided."[2]

In America in the 1890s, the so-called yellow press of Hearst and Pulitzer was notorious not only for sensationalistic coverage of the Cuban rebellion and the subsequent Spanish-American War, but also for staging many of the spectacles they reported. When in 1896 the illustrator Fredric Remington complained to Hearst from Havana that nothing was happening, Hearst reportedly responded, "You furnish the pictures and I'll furnish the war."[3] To keep his promise, Hearst filled his front page with pictures of Spanish atrocities at the same time that he started the modern sports page.[4] Both Hearst and Pulitzer made the news they reported by sending reporters on special spy missions, by leading rescue campaigns of Cuban ladies, or by using their own yachts—carrying their reporters—to capture Spanish refugees.

REPORTERS AS ACTORS

These spectacles often featured the reporter himself as their chief actor. During the international wars between the Civil War and World War I, the foreign correspondent came into being as a professional writer with a public persona. Bylines changed from "from our own correspondent" to the attribution of personal names, and headlines sometimes included the name of the reporter, as in the case of a celebrity like Crane: "STEPHEN CRANE AT THE FRONT FOR THE WORLD," "STEPHEN CRANE'S VIVID STORY OF THE BATTLE OF SAN JUAN," and "STEPHEN CRANE SKETCHES THE COMMON SOLDIER."[5] Reporters often made themselves or their colleagues the heroes of their stories and the act of reporting the main plot. This focus turned writing into a strenuous activity and the reporter into a virile figure who rivaled the soldiers. If the private, Henry Fleming, tries to become a spectator of the same battle he fights, reporters, the professional spectators, often tried to become actors by engaging in combat. Crane himself both played and parodied the figure of the heroic correspondent by flaunting his indifference to bullets under fire and by capturing a Puerto Rican town in a mock invasion. The theatrical style of *The Red Badge of Courage* anticipates the aggrandizement of the act of reporting to overshadow the action on the battlefield.

By dramatizing the exploits of the reporter, newspapers transformed political and military conflicts in foreign colonies into romantic adventures in exotic landscapes. In addition, Crane suggests in his novel *Active Service*—based on his experience in the Greco-Turkish War—that the reporter also provided an important spectatorial function for the soldiers on the field, who

> when they go away to the fighting ground, out of the sight, out of the hearing of the world known to them and are eager to perform feats of war in this new place they feel an absolute longing for a spectator. . . . The war correspondent arises, then, to become a sort of cheap telescope for the people at home; further still, there have been fights where the eyes of a solitary man were the eyes of the world; one spectator whose business it was to transfer, according to his ability, his visual impressions to other minds.[6]

This "cheap telescope" proved especially important on the battlefield of colonial territories, where enemy combatants often were both physically and ideologically invisible. Reports from Cuba commented on the difficulty American troops had in seeing the Spanish fighters, who sniped at them through the thick brush. After Spain surrendered, America's former allies, the Cubans and even more so the Filipinos, turned their guerrilla warfare against the Americans now occupying their lands. Whereas the European Spaniards were represented as equal, if hated, foes, the Cuban and Filipino guerrillas, even as allies, were represented not as soldiers fighting a real war but as criminal elements to subdue.[7] In the face of such invisible and shifting allies and enemies, the political context of the war often blurred. The reporter redrew the contours of a foreign terrain by dramatizing American action and identity in the eyes of the audience at home rather than in relation to a shadowy and less than human enemy. The promise of being seen through the medium of the newspaper compensates for the confusion and the fear of not seeing.

In *The Red Badge of Courage,* Crane had already developed the mechanisms of this cheap telescope by rendering the enemy invisible on the battlefield of the Civil War and by making the soldier's identity more contingent on an audience than on conflict with the foe. Many of Crane's newspaper reports call attention to the spectacular nature of the battles through techniques similar to those we have seen in his novel. In Crane's story of the Rough Riders' "gallant blunder," for example, their noise and bravado appear to be directed more toward making an impression on a domestic audience than toward using effective strategy against the enemy, and in his vivid report of the regulars charging up San Juan Hill, Crane offers the readers cues for cheering, as though he were describing a football game.[8]

If his newspaper reports utilize this cheap telescope, many of Crane's later stories about war test its ramifications and its limits. Much of his late fiction explores the boundary line between action and spectatorship and the consequences of crossing it. The correspondent in "Death and the Child," for example, loses his mind when he tries to step over that line; he takes up arms to join the battle, only to hallucinate that the gun is strangling him. In "The Open Boat," the correspondent finds himself thrust into the role of actor in a classic adventure tale, only to share impotence and blindness with the other men in the boat. . . .

The link between Crane's revision of the Civil War and his representation of international warfare in the 1890s may help explain the unique position of *The Red Badge of Courage* in literary history, not only as the classic novel about the American Civil War but also as a paradigm of the modern American war novel. The popularity of Crane's book in both England and America in the 1890s can be understood in the context of the heightened militarism in both cultures, enacted on the battlefields of colonial territories. If those British reviewers were correct who read *The Red Badge of Courage* as a critique of jingoism, of the spectatorial lust that facilitated imperial warfare, its critique must be an imminent one that emerges from a narrative structure engaged in producing the spectacle of modern warfare.[9]

In his legacy to the century he did not live to see, Crane not only redefined the war novel through the focus on the psyche of the individual soldier but also "invented the persona of the war correspondent for the novelist"[10] of the twentieth century. The components of this figure who straddles the boundary line between spectator and actor are already present in *The Red Badge of Courage.* There Crane not only outlined a hero and a narrative strategy to be fleshed out by American writers from Ernest Hemingway to Norman Mailer, but his revision of the Civil War also shaped both the experience and the representation of those remote wars that American writers have pursued throughout the twentieth century. It is Crane's anticipation of the modern spectacle of war, more than his historical veracity, that allowed Hemingway to write in 1942 that *The Red Badge of Courage* was the only enduring "real literature of our Civil War."

REFERENCES

1. J.A. Hobson, *Imperialism: A Study* (1902; reprinted Ann Arbor: University of Michigan Press, 1972), p. 215.

2. Phillip Knightley, *The First Casualty: From Crimea to Vietnam: The War Correspondent as Hero, Propagandist and Myth Maker* (New York: Harcourt, Brace, Jovanovich, 1975), p. 42.

3. Frank Luther Mott, *American Journalism: 1690–1960* (New York: 1962), p. 529.

4. John Higham, "The Re-Orientation of American Culture in the 1890's," in *Writing American History: Essays in Modern Scholarship* (Bloomington: Indiana University Press, 1970), p. 84.

5. Stephen Crane, *Reports of War,* ed. Fredson Bowers (Charlottesville: University of Virginia Press, 1971), pp. 487, 492, 495.

6. Stephen Crane, *The Third Violet and Active Service,* ed. Fredson Bowers (Charlottesville: University Press of Virginia, 1976), p. 172.

7. David Axeen, "'Heroes of the Engine Room: American 'Civilization' and the War with Spain,'" *American Quarterly 36* (Fall 1984) pp. 499–510.

8. Crane, *Reports of War,* pp. 146, 154–65.

9. For examples of this reading, see Richard Weatherford, ed., *Stephen Crane: The Critical Heritage* (London: Routledge & Kegan Paul, 1973), pp. 99, 105, 127.

10. Martin Green, *The Great American Adventure* (Boston: Beacon Press, 1984), p. 169.

CHAPTER 3

"The Open Boat"

READINGS ON
STEPHEN CRANE

"The Open Boat" Is a Study of Man Against Nature

E.R. Hagemann

E.R. Hagemann writes that the theme of the "The Open Boat" centers on man's confrontation with nature and the realization that nature is neither hostile nor benevolent, merely indifferent. Hagemann sees the characters in the story as interpreters, who learn a bit about the world by accident and come back to the reader to tell their tale. Critic E.R. Hagemann has coedited a collection of Crane's work with R.W. Stallman, *The New York City Sketches of Stephen Crane and Related Pieces.*

Toward the end of "Stephen Crane's Own Story," a newspaper account of the sinking of the filibustering S.S. *Commodore*, the newspaperman says:

> The history of life in an open boat for thirty hours would no doubt be instructive for the young, but none is to be told here now. For my part I would prefer to tell the story at once, because from it would shine the splendid manhood of Captain Edward Murphy and of William Higgins, the oiler, but let it suffice at this time to say that when we were swamped in the surf and making the best of our way toward the shore the captain gave orders amid the wildness of the breakers as clearly as if he had been on the quarter deck of a battleship.[1]

Undoubtedly, Crane was already planning his fictional version—he says he "would prefer to tell the story at once." Furthermore, he included the title within the first sentence, i.e., "The Open Boat.". . .

THE CLIMAX

Precisely mid-point in the story (in section 4), there occurs among the four occupants of the ten-foot dinghy a spirited conversation concerning a dimly apprehended man on the beach.

Excerpted from E.R. Hagemann, "'Sadder Than the End': Another Look at 'The Open Boat,'" in *Stephen Crane in Transition: Centenary Essays,* edited by Joseph Katz (DeKalb: Northern Illinois University Press, 1972). Copyright ©1972 by Northern Illinois University Press. Reprinted by permission of the publisher.

"Look at the fellow with the flag. Maybe he ain't waving it!"

"That ain't a flag, is it? That's his coat. Why, certainly, that's his coat."

"So it is; it's his coat. He's taken it off and is waving it around his head. But would you look at him swing it!"

Metaphorically, the man has a message for the four men, incomprehensible to them at that moment, although it should not have been for, after all, they had been previously forced to take the boat back out to sea. The signalman also has a message for the reader, incomprehensible as it is at this moment despite the foreshadowings given by Crane.

The appearance of signalman mid-way in the story indicates its careful construction. His frantic, if not demonic, waving is the climax. Before sighting him, the four men—pained by the rowing, discomfited by the waves, and chilled by the cold—were confident, despite an unsuccessful attempt to run through the surf, that they would ultimately make it without undue difficulty. They should not have been; their circumstances warranted no such confidence.

Three times in the first paragraph, fourteen times in all in section 1, Crane mentions or alludes to the waves, beyond and through which these men must go to gain the shore—that beautiful, macadam-hard, gently-inclined stretch of sand just south of Daytona. Looking out from the boat, there are always the waves; the horizon narrows and widens, dips and rises; "at all times its edge . . . jagged with waves that [seem] thrust up in points like rocks"; each wave-top is "a problem in small boat navigation." Nature, at her most unpleasant, allows the men a glimpse of the shore, reminds them of her indifferent strength as if they needed to be reminded. For they have escaped, in the "greys of dawn," the fate of seven of their shipmates as "a stump of a top-mast with a white ball on it" slashed at the waves and then went "low and lower, and down."

The sinking of the luckless S.S. *Commodore* is the fact, and I suggest that Crane indicates this by alluding to it so soon in the story. Now these four men are *after the fact,* on one level of meaning, and they must get to shore before they are bested by "these problems in white water" and "the snarling of the crests." The correspondent and the cook argue about the difference between a life-saving station and house of refuge. The cook insists that a crew from the house of refuge will pick them up as soon as they are sighted.[2] The correspondent insists that a house of refuge does not have a crew. He is correct.[5]

Abruptly, Billy Higgins, the oiler, says, "Well, we're not there yet, anyhow." Indeed they are not; the cook shifts his argument; the oiler repeats, "We're not there yet." What the oiler says is true in several ways: they have not gained the shore—far from it; nor have they garnered the "direct personal knowledge" to be able to say, "I've been there," which implies experience and thereby allows them to become interpreters. Billy's words foreshadow his own end and make all the more ironic a third level of meaning—not one of them has met Death. They had seen Him in the "greys of dawn," though, and seen His attribute, "the white ball" on the mast, in that carefully arranged canvas Crane paints for the reader.

NATURE TOYS WITH THE MEN

In section 2, the occupants in the "freighted" boat (figuratively laden with death and violence) oscillate between hope and despair with Crane carefully introducing each element. The cook mentions the on-shore wind—they wouldn't have a "show" without it; the oiler and the correspondent heartily agree. Captain Murphy laughs away their optimism; his "crew" is silent: "the ethics of their condition was decidedly against any open suggestion of hopelessness." Then Murphy soothes them, saying, "Oh well, . . . we'll get ashore all right." Immediately, the oiler agrees, but only if the wind holds; the cook agrees, but only if they don't catch "hell in the surf."

Nature is toying with them; Crane is toying with the reader. "Canton-flannel" gulls, ordinarily a welcome sight to the sailor, fly about the men or ride the waves. The gulls come close and stare "with black, bead-like eyes . . . uncanny and sinister in their unblinking scrutiny." One gull perches on the captain's head! Seated in the bow of the dinghy, the smallest of all boats that puts to sea, the Captain with the gull atop him is a perfect duplication of the image seen when the *Commodore* went down: "a stump of a topmast with a white ball on it." In this masterful bit of ambiguous foreshadowing, Murphy is the mast and the gull is the ball; the men in the "freighted" craft sense Death because the sea bird strikes them somehow as "gruesome and ominous." They breathe easier when the Captain waves it away, and they set to rowing and rowing and rowing and oscillate to a feeling of optimism, as adjacent "brown mats" of seaweed inform them they are "making progress slowly toward the land."

HOPE

Their optimism increases when the Mosquito Inlet light-house appears like "a small still thing on the edge of the swaying horizon," having the dimensions and forcefulness of "the point of a pin." That they could see the light, 159 feet above mean high water, was cause for hope: probably they were no more than fifteen or sixteen nautical miles from shore.[4] Will they make it, is the question. "If this wind [an on-shore wind] holds and the boat don't swamp [in the surf], we can't do much else" says the Captain. Crane skillfully balances the wind and the surf against the lighthouse. Hope is strong aboard the "wee thing" wallowing "at the mercy of five oceans."

> "Bail her, cook," said the captain, serenely.
> "All right, Captain," said the cheerful cook.

They have overlooked the gull. They have been *gulled*!

Captain Murphy wishes for a sail (section 3), and almost magically his overcoat is rigged to an oar and the little boat makes "good way" as the oiler steers and sculls with the other oar, such good way that the lighthouse becomes "an upright shadow on the sky" and the land seems "a long black shadow on the sea," adumbrations of the ultimate tragedy. This stretch of shore is not a welcoming and verdant shore. Crane renders this ironically apparent when the cook suggests that they should be opposite New Smyrna, Florida. Surely the sounding of this New World name (almost a cognomen for a town of about 500 souls) conjures a vision of the flourishing seaport of the old Ottoman Empire.[5] Even the life-saving station seems to have been recently abandoned, and the cook so informs the Captain who merely says, "Did they?" The wind slowly dies, Crane briefly alludes to the foundering of the *Commodore*, and the crew take to the oars. They make good progress; they cannot be concerned with irony. They make out a house on the shore—the house of refuge for the homeless and destitute of the sea. The lighthouse rears high; "slowly and beautifully" the land looms out of the Atlantic.

Nevertheless, there are discords: the sound of the surf and the veering of the wind to the southeast. They cannot make the lighthouse now. They are not discouraged—far from it.

They swing the dinghy "a little more north" and watch the shore grow. They are quietly cheerful. "In an hour, perhaps, they would be ashore." That simple! A relatively easy matter of a few hours at sea! The correspondent passes out cigars, and the "four waifs" puff away and ride "impudently" in their little boat, forgetful of the earlier argument over a life-saving station and a house of refuge. They willingly pin their

---

"THE OPEN BOAT" REJECTS CHRISTIANITY

It is common to interpret Stephen Crane's short story "The Open Boat" as a naturalistic reading of life, as the author's "apostrophe to the new Darwinian cosmos of blind forces—of chance and cosmic indifference" (Maxwell Geismar, *Rebels and Ancestors*, p. 99). Few will quarrel with this judgment. What may have been overlooked is the degree to which the tale seems to invert conventional Christian motifs and rituals while it traces the development of a new religion.

There would be nothing in this to occasion surprise. Crane toys with inversions of Christian themes in his novel *The Red Badge of Courage* and in his short religious poems. But "The Open Boat" may be read in such a way that mockery of traditional Christianity, although never explicitly, is woven into almost every event....

In the story's climax, the men learn that nothing is outside them except the projection of themselves and their needs. Their plea to the universe is lost in remote and indifferent space. From the answer of a "high cold star on a winter's night" they know at last the truth about the mechanistic cosmos in which they live.

They are saved finally.... Their savior is unadorned, divested of anything that could show office, dignity, or status. He is "naked as a tree in winter, but a halo was about his head, and he shone like a saint." He is surrounded on shore by people who have "all the remedies sacred to their minds." It is right that these should take the form of clothing, blankets, and coffee-pots—ritual requirements in the religion which finds nothing important beyond man.

A new religion requires new apostles. The three men left alive have learned that the world is indifferent and that men must supply their own needs. But they have also learned that brotherhood and courage make life endurable. They are ready now to be the hierophants of a new religion, and its true interpreters.

Robert Meyers, "Crane's *The Open Boat*," *The Explicator*, April 1963.

hopes on the latter; forgetful, if they in fact knew, that they are "waifs"; blown by the wind, wanderers, discarded human goods from a sunk ship, owner unknown.

Captain Murphy reminds them, remarking to the cook that "there don't seem to be any signs of life about your house of refuge." The surf's roar is plain to hear; everyone is suddenly positive they will swamp. In what amounts to a parenthetical aside, Crane says that "there was not a life-saving station within twenty miles in either direction."[6] Understandably, their "light-heartedness of a former time" has "completely faded." No boat is seen pulling to succor them. They had better make a run through the surf; the oiler turns the boat "straight for the shore," amidst some "admonitions" and "reflections" with a "good deal of rage" in them.

> If I am going to be drowned—if I am going to be drowned—if I am going to be drowned, why, in the name of the seven made gods who rule the sea, was I allowed to come thus far and contemplate sand and trees? Was I brought here merely to have my nose dragged away as I was about to nibble the sacred cheese of life? It is preposterous!

It *is*, no one will deny, seemingly preposterous to be so close. But they are not *there* yet, to recall the oiler's words; and to have made it through the surf on the first run was not to be their lot. Fate, . . . and Atropos have other plans, namely, interpretation. Aware now that they wouldn't last three minutes in such a surf, they take the dinghy to sea again. Wind, wave, and tide fight for possession of the craft; it gains a little northward.

They spot a man, a "little black figure," running on the shore. He waves; they tie a bath towel to a stick and wave back. Another man appears; he, too, waves. A resort hotel omnibus appears, and yet another man stands on the steps and waves. And we are brought to mid-point of the story, the signaling episode, the climax, told by Crane from the point of view of the four "waifs" in the dinghy in two full pages of dialogue, without tag lines, description, or exposition, to point up the irony.

"What's the idiot with the coat mean? What's he signaling, anyhow?" demands one waif. A perfectly marvelous question. The answers are various: he is telling them to go north; he thinks the waifs are fishing and is giving them "a merry hand." Another waif says, "He don't mean anything. He's just playing." That, most assuredly, he is not doing. As I interpret it, what he is telling them is this: *you can't come in yet; you can't get through so easily; you stay outside there and suffer; when your time comes, you can come through; sorry, but that is the way it is.* In the growing dusk, the four men helplessly sit in the boat. When the spray hits them, they swear "like men who were being branded." They row and they row and they row. The lighthouse disappears from the southern horizon. And again the "if I am going to be drowned" motif enters this section, stressing the structure within the section and within the story and stressing the meaning. In this reappearance of "if I am going to be drowned," Crane pointedly, yet subtly, omits the statement "It is preposterous" and all that follows relative to Fate. Their situation is no *longer* preposterous in the "freighted" dinghy, and they see a glimmer of what is in store for them. A different mood is among them, and Crane employs appropriate language: the captain is "patient" when he issues orders; the crew's voices are "weary" and "low" in reply; the evening is "quiet"—a prelude to the morning to come; and all but the oarsman lie "heavily and listlessly" in the dinghy....

What was buoyant optimism and hope in the earlier part is now a long night "on the sea in an open boat." Two lights, one to the north (one is tempted to think it is the St. Augustine Lighthouse) and the other to the south (Mosquito Inlet Lighthouse), are "the furniture of the world" and remind us of the argument about the house of refuge and the life-saving station.[7] Only the man at the oars is awake; the others are sleeping, a word that Crane used, naturally enough, time and again with variations in this passage; for now, having attained a dim perception of what is in store for them, they need the preparatory sleep.

SADDER THAN THE END

The correspondent keeps the boat headed and regards the sleeping oiler and cook, arms wrapped about each other, there in the bottom: "babes of the sea." This womb image, shortly to be repeated, wryly recalls the jauntily oblivious "waifs" in section 3 as they "impudently" rode the waves. Such a difference now. Writes Crane: "The wind had a voice as it came over the waves, and it was sadder than the end." Nothing could be more felicitous at this point in the story. The end, of course, is Death for all of us (and them, too), and this is sad; sadder yet is to remember what we did not know we knew, as Robert Frost says; sadder yet is to become "interpreters" before Death and to carry this burden and tell of its meaning to the uninitiated. This sentence also sums up the ordeal of the correspondent and the oiler as they meekly and steadily spell each other at the oars throughout the night. No arguments or petulant comments; rather compassion and contriteness if a wave but splashes into the boat. Dim as their perception of the ways of existence may be, "the subtle brotherhood" of men at sea, spoken of by Crane in section 3, indicates obedience and grace of conduct as they approach what is "sadder than the end."

Suddenly there appears the predatory shark, the largest fish of all, swishing through the water "like blue flame," speeding "like a shadow" ahead or astern, port or starboard. Its fin, knifing the water, leaving "a gleaming trail of phosphorescence," literally draws a magic circle around the dinghy. The waifs must stay in the boat, perform, carry on. This particular shark is not a predator—it will not plunder; it is, Crane says, a "biding thing," and the correspondent, without horror, simply looks "dully" at the sea and swears "in an undertone." He is not vindictive; he merely wishes he were not alone "with the thing." But his companions are sleeping their preparatory sleep.

The final iteration of the "if I am going to be drowned" motif opens section 6. This seems a normal thought on the part of the lonely correspondent and directs the reader to compare this third repetition with the previous two. The first expressed the collective emotions of the four waifs; the second (more a refrain than anything else and assigned to no one waif) expressed the mood of the moment; the third expresses the meditations of the correspondent and expands them into a fear of drowning, "an abominable injustice" to a man who has worked "so hard, so hard." He wants so to live, to survive. To drown would be "a crime most unnatural." To this point in his life, apparently, the correspondent, unlike his creator and his counterpart, has not given time and effort to wrestling with the idea of an unjust, i.e., unlawful universe. Only in the physical realms, in the sciences (for example, astronomy), is the universe lawful; here lies what Thomas Paine once called the "true theology" of man.

Injustice is not for the correspondent. He wishes for recognition of himself as an entity. But:

When it occurs to a man that nature does not regard him as

important, and that she feels she would not maim the universe by disposing of him, he at first wishes to throw bricks
at the temple, and he hates deeply the fact that there are no
bricks and no temples. Any visible expression of nature
would surely be pelleted with his jeers.

NATURE'S INDIFFERENCE

Crane at last has tentatively stated the theme of the story: the
indifference of nature to man's struggles. If there be "no tangible thing to hoot," muses the correspondent, at least he
wishes to confront "a personification" and plead, "Yes, but I
love myself." The reply is the symbolic "high cold star," and
the correspondent knows "the pathos of his situation": to be
faced by an indifferent but ever-watchful Nature. A vagrant
ditty from his childhood about "A soldier of the Legion" who
is dying in Algiers—where there are also sand and trees (to
recall the motif)—enters the correspondent's memory and
enforces the delineation of the theme. As a child, he had
never regarded this death as important, notwithstanding
that it was dinned into his boyish mind by "myriads of his
school-fellows." He had been indifferent to such a death; it
was something less important to him than "the breaking of
a pencil's point." Now, at the oars with the "cold star" above
him, he is very sorry "for the soldier of the Legion." Crane's
irony is subtle: the correspondent's dinning in the presence
of Nature has produced indifference; the schoolboys' dinning the song in his presence had produced indifference.
However, in his desert ordeal the soldier had had a comrade
to hold his hand; of this small boon the correspondent on the
morrow cannot be sure.

Captain Murphy and the correspondent briefly discuss
the shark, who has departed the vicinity, evidently "bored at
the delay." The oiler and the correspondent spell each other
at the oars; the cook lends a hand and works the dinghy farther out to sea, only to be driven back. The shark returns.
The correspondent assumes the thwart and works the
dinghy outward. Then this cogent close to the section:

At last there was a short conversation.
"Billie! . . . Billie, will you spell me?"
"Sure," said the oiler.

There is much more here than a simple question-and-
answer; present are foreshadowing and irony and a signpost
planted by Crane to direct the reader to the violent finish of

the story. What the correspondent (who "loves" himself and feels "sorry" for the dying soldier) has really asked the oiler is for Billie to serve in his place, to replace him, when the dinghy makes its ultimate run through the surf and when "the old ninny-woman Fate" (in three persons) decides finally the destiny of these four humans who have been wallowing in the sea under the "cold star." There is something disconcerting about the oiler's prompt affirmative.

It is time for the final journey through the combers, after which they will be *there*. The preparations are over. Crane opens the section with the same gray cast that was present in the first paragraph of the story. On the dunes appear "many little black cottages" and "a tall white windmill" which rears above them as they plunge for the beach; these provide the focus for Crane's specific statement of the theme of "The Open Boat."

> This tower was a giant, standing with its back to the plight of the ants. It represented in a degree, to the correspondent, the serenity of nature amid the struggles of the individual—nature in the wind, and nature in the vision of men. She did not seem cruel to him then, nor beneficent, nor treacherous, nor wise. But she was indifferent, flatly indifferent. It is, perhaps, plausible that a man in this situation, impressed with the unconcern of the universe, should see the innumerable flaws of his life. . . .

DEATH AS A PHENOMENON OF NATURE

The Captain orders, "don't jump until she swamps sure" ; the oiler (as he had in section 1) has the oars, and he backs in toward "the lonely and indifferent shore." The correspondent's thoughts touch briefly on the drowning motif (what "a shame" it would be) just before the first comber smashes them; they survive this as they do the second crest. The third wave, "huge, furious, implacable . . . fairly swallows" them, and the men go into the icy water: the oiler swimming strongly in the lead, the cook using the life-belt, the Captain clinging to the overturned dinghy. Three times Crane describes the shore, the representational *there* to these waifs—representational to them as having "a certain immovable quality," as being set before them like "a bit of scenery on a stage," and as "a picture" in "a gallery," a scene from Algiers perhaps. The thought of the dying legionnaire haunts the correspondent as does the thought of drowning. "Can it be possible? Can it be possible? Can it be possible?" echo and balance his previous cadence, "If I am going to be drowned." A perverse observation adds, "perhaps an individual must consider his own death to be the final phenomenon of nature."

The four waifs struggle mightily there in the surf. Finally an actor appears on the stage-like shore: a man running, undressing rapidly as he runs. Miraculously the surf flings the correspondent over the dangerous, overturned boat and into shallow water. He is not safely *there* yet; now he fights the undertow. The naked man-actor comes into the water, rescues the cook, and wades toward the correspondent who sees "a halo about his head." He shines "like a saint." There is something suggestively comic about the rescue here as the man heaves and tugs at the correspondent, but the comedy fades when the man points "a swift finger" and runs at the correspondent's command. "In the shallows, face downward, lay the oiler. His forehead touched sand that was periodically, between each wave, clear of the sea."

Billy Higgins, oiler aboard the S.S. *Commodore,* who had earlier implacably said, "We're not there yet," has arrived *there,* not as an interpreter, but as "a still and dripping shape" being carried to the grave in the midst of "the welcome of the land" (the people with restoratives and blankets). The survivors are *there*; indifferent Nature is transformed into benevolent Nature, and now "the old ninny-woman Fate" has extracted her toll.

> When it came night, the white waves paced to and fro in the moonlight, and the wind brought the sound of the great sea's voice to the men on shore, and they felt that they could then be interpreters.

A FRESH PAIR OF EYES

The "voice" here—a coda surely—sounds the notes of the other wind (in section 5) which was "sadder than the end." And we are brought to the final word, "interpreters." Of what are these men, no longer waifs, interpreters? The necessity was to struggle against an indifferent nature. But also much more than that, for this seems almost absurd in its simplicity. We must return to the epigraph, "A TALE INTENDED TO BE AFTER THE FACT: BEING THE / EXPERIENCE OF FOUR MEN FROM THE SUNK STEAMER / COMMODORE," and to the discussion early in this paper to glean the many complexities involved.[8] Crane in this story is seeking the universal fact of existence subsequent to the particular fact of the sinking of the *Commodore.* "The Open Boat" is his retrospection *(ex post facto)* and, as I have said, the reader's, too. From this retrospection emerges his (and the reader's) personal knowledge which makes plain the ultimate meaning of experience. Made plain, too, is the form or structure. Significantly, Crane in the epigraph speaks of the experience of four men; so Billy Higgins is included. To sum up, the totality of experience for the living and the dead is: existence. These three men have become brothers to Henry Fleming whose journey to the other side is so brilliantly explicated in the final paragraphs of *The Red Badge of Courage.* Captain Murphy, the cook, and the correspondent, in their journey from "the greys of dawn" to the "welcome of the land," went on yet another journey—a private one to another land of There. The length of that journey, the time consumed is of little import. Within its duration, they learned a little bit, gained an "accidental education" (to use Henry Adams's doctrine, which in the final analysis is a goodly amount) in and about courage. Not heroism and all its ritualistically empty gestures, but *courage.* They have returned to the same unjust but nevertheless welcome world that so outrageously allowed the S.S. *Commodore* to sink, but now they view it with a "fresh pair of eyes."

Indeed, to be an "interpreter" is "sadder than the end." Another allusion to Henry Adams is fitting: the correspondent's education began and ended in the open boat; what he has learned and communicated in "The Open Boat" is no doubt "instructive for the young."

NOTES

1. Joseph Katz, *The Portable Stephen Crane* (New York: Viking Press, 1969), p. 342; reprinted from the *New York Press,* 7 January 1897, p. 1. At this point, I wish to express my appreciation to Prof. R.W. Stallman for his remarks on "The Open Boat" (*Stephen Crane: An Omnibus* [New York: Alfred A. Knopf, 1952], pp. 415–20); they are very suggestive. In some ways, but certainly not all, my essay is a commentary on those remarks.

2. Maintained by the United States Life-Saving Service, this house of refuge is on the beach outside Mosquito Lagoon, just north of Mosquito Inlet Light (known as Ponce de Leon Light on present-day charts). In 1897, this house was in the 7th District, United States Life-Saving Service.

3. The Life-Saving Service then maintained three types of installations: life-saving stations, which had a crew and life-saving ap-

pliances of all kinds; houses of refuge, supplied with boats, provisions, etc., in the charge of keepers but without crews; and life-boat stations.

4. The light at Mosquito Inlet was fixed white, used oil as an illuminant, and was visible at night to a maximum of 18 3/4 nautical miles. The tower was red brick and conical in shape; there were three brick dwellings near it. Established in 1887 and given Number 1059, the tower was about one mile to the north and west of the entrance to Mosquito Inlet and 52 miles SSE from the St. Augustine Lighthouse (*List of Lights and Fog Signals on the Atlantic and Gulf Coasts . . . to . . . March 1, 1907* [Washington, 1907], pp. 206–7).

5. About 13 miles SSE of Daytona Beach; the name was changed to New Smyrna Beach in 1937.

6. As a matter of fact, there was no life-saving station in the area at all. The next house of refuge north was at Smiths Creek, 20 miles south of Matanzas Inlet; south, at Chester Shoal, 11 miles north of Cape Kennedy. See *Annual Report of the Operations of the United States Life-Saving Service for . . . 1897*, Treasury Department Document No. 1996 (Washington, 1898), p. 369.

7. It is unlikely that the correspondent saw the St. Augustine Light; what he saw was probably a light in Daytona Beach or possibly north of the town. The tower of the St. Augustine Light was 161 feet high with a fixed white light, varied by a white flash every three minutes. It was visible for 18 3/4 nautical miles.

8. As originally printed in *Scribner's Magazine* in 1897.

"The Open Boat" Is a Traditional Sea Story

Bert Bender

Bert Bender teaches at Arizona State University, has been a commercial fisherman, and is the author of the book *Sea Brothers: The Tradition of American Sea Fiction from* Moby Dick *to the Present,* from which the following article is excerpted. Bender argues that in "The Open Boat" Crane follows in the tradition of other great sea writers such as Joseph Conrad and Herman Melville. Crane's correspondent learns something valuable about humanity's relationship to nature through his experience on the open water.

Stephen Crane was never a working seaman and so cannot be placed squarely within the tradition of American writers who were "sea-brothers." But on the basis of his very brief experience at sea he wrote one of the greatest sea stories of all time and centered it on the idea of brotherhood at sea. Few short stories in any language have won as high a place in world literature as has "The Open Boat." Its universal appeal is that it illustrates, simply and profoundly, "the essentials of life, like a symbolic tale," as Joseph Conrad assessed it. There can be no question that the experience Crane recreated in his story brought home to him what was essential in his own life. The ordeal in the dinghy was "the best experience of his life" because it brought him to feel "the subtle brotherhood of men that was [there] established on the sea" ("The Open Boat," pt. 3). A year after the incident, he dedicated *The Open Boat and Other Stories* to his three comrades in the dinghy. And in Cora Crane's report of his last hours, three and a half years after the incident, the profound personal significance of his experience resounds: "My husband's brain is never at rest. He lives over everything in

Reprinted from chapter 5 of Bert Bender, *Sea Brothers: The Tradition of American Sea Fiction from* Moby-Dick *to the Present.* Copyright ©1988 by the University of Pennsylvania Press. Reprinted by permission of the publisher.

dreams and talks aloud constantly. It is too awful to hear him try to change places in the 'Open Boat'."

Crane certainly idealized the working seaman in his portrayal of William Higgins. Billie the oiler "had worked a double watch in the engine room of the ship" before it sank, and then, in the dinghy, his tireless labor and his expertise as a seaman were instrumental in his comrades' survival. "A wily surfman," Billie saves them twice. First, when the dinghy had been caught "in a turmoil of foam" too far out for them to have swum ashore, he advised the captain to put to sea again: then "this oiler, by a series of quick miracles and fast and steady oarsmanship, turned the boat in the middle of the surf, and took her safely to sea." And he saves them a second time, in the final crisis, by swinging the boat about so as to "keep her head-on to the seas and back her in." In his presentation of Billie's actions and through such devices as the refrain "the oiler rowed, and then the correspondent rowed, and then the oiler rowed," Crane emphasizes that Billie's steady, simple labor is the tangible basis for his role here as a savior, whose "miracles" of seamanship complement Crane's idealized imagery of him as "the weary-faced oiler smil[ing] in full sympathy" and asking "meekly," "will you spell me for a while?"

Crane's portrayal of Billie, the simple, working seaman, clearly expresses his sympathy with the democratic ideal of the sailor before the mast that figures so crucially in the tradition of American sea fiction. And to judge from the famous photograph of Crane aboard the *Three Friends* (barefoot and spread-legged, the image of a swashbuckling sailor) or from his signing himself, "Stephen Crane, able seaman S.S. *Commodore*," one might even entertain, for an instant, the idea that Crane might have been a sailor had his life's circumstances been different. . . .

GETTING IT RIGHT

In writing the story of "the best experience of his life," Crane wanted desperately to get it "*right*," from Captain Murphy's point of view. Of course he wanted to please Murphy, whom he revered in the story and honored in his dedication to *The Open Boat and Other Stories*. But he seems mainly to have wanted Murphy's assurance, as an experienced seaman, that he had handled the sea materials correctly. He was obviously proud of having signed on as an able seaman and of "doing a seaman's work . . . well," as the cook reported. The experience meant far too much to him to risk having his story discredited as a landlubber's view of the sea. He needed no assurance that he was a brilliant reporter. With Murphy's assurance that "you've got it right, Steve. That is just how it happened," he could confidently claim—like any experienced seaman in the tradition of American sea fiction—that he had been there, that his story was authentic. Thus in his subtitle for "The Open Boat," "A Tale Intended to Be After the Fact: Being the Experience of Four Men from the Sunk Steamer *Commodore*," there is something like the young Melville's claim in the first sentence of *Typee* that the story of his "six months at sea!" would not resemble the tales of "state-room sailors" about "the privations and hardships of the sea" on "a fourteen-days' passage across the Atlantic." As Crane wrote, "In a ten-foot dinghy one can get an idea of the resources of the sea in the line of waves that is not probable to the average experience, which is never at sea in a dinghy." No seaman has ever faulted Crane's presentation of nautical reality in "The Open Boat." Only an occasional unenlightened critic has argued that Crane failed "to achieve circumstantial verisimilitude" in his story, that the men's "physical hardships" in the dinghy were "grossly exaggerated."

But if Captain Murphy could assure Crane that he had got the facts of their experience right, it would take a much more sensitive reader—one like Captain [Joseph] Conrad—to appreciate Crane's success in launching his story immediately into the much higher realm of experience that is indicated in the first sentence by "sky." From this first moment, after which there will be considerable scanning of the heavens, "The Open Boat" proceeds as a traditional sea journey to knowledge, and the knowledge it attains is equally as mysterious or religious as that envisioned in other great American sea journeys—in Cooper's *Sea Lions*, for example, or Melville's *Mardi* and *Moby-Dick*, or Hemingway's *Old Man and the Sea*. The great difference between Crane's sea journey and these others is that, in its more purely autobiographical approach, it dramatizes an experience like those William James would describe two years after Crane's death in *The Varieties of Religious Experience*. The most intense moment of this experience in the story occurs in part 6 when the correspondent, having discovered "the pathos of his situation," has a vision, or what James

Joyce might have called an "epiphany": a verse "mysteriously" entered his head, and he "plainly saw" a comrade, the soldier in Algiers whose death prefigures Billie's. This explicitly visionary moment is exactly the kind of "religious experience" that James had in mind in defining such experiences as "*the feelings, acts, and experiences of individual men in their solitude, so far as they apprehend themselves to stand in relation to whatever they may consider the divine*"; and he defined "divine" as that "primal reality" that "the individual feels impelled to respond to solemnly and gravely, and neither by a curse nor a jest." Such experiences, James was almost "appalled" to discover, involved much "sentimentality" and "emotionality," and he realized that "in all these matters of sentiment one must have 'been there' one's self in order to understand them.". . .

Brotherhood

But if "The Open Boat" is a traditional sea journey that attains an unconventional sense of religious values or of "primal reality," as James might have preferred to put it, the values themselves are scarcely new. Indeed, centering as they do on a "brotherhood of men," they cohere in Crane's imagination in a way that reflects the traditional Christian realities that he knew as a boy. In his actual experience in the boat, he found a real captain who was also a kind of Father, a brother in Billie, who was also miraculously and "meekly" a kind of Son, and a "mysterious," ghostly sense that they were one. All this not despite but rather because of the bitter sense of his refrain "God is cold. . . . God is cold. . . . God is cold" (in his poem "A Man Adrift on a Slim Spar," which he wrote at the same time that he was writing "The Open Boat").

Perhaps it is because Crane has come to be identified with some of his more famous expressions ("God Lay Dead in Heaven" or "God is cold") that there is considerable disagreement about the values he envisions in "The Open Boat," or even about whether the story affirms any values. One critic, for example, writing from a conventional religious point of view, complained that "in Crane's view evidently no valid insight or awareness . . . can be derived from human experience." And, focusing on the story's initial sense that "none of them *knew*" (my emphasis), another critic has argued that the story's "epistemological emphasis" points to "man's limited capacities for knowing reality."

Such interpretations obscure Crane's efforts to show how his correspondent did come to know reality (in the ultimate sense that James had in mind when he wrote *The Varieties of Religious Experience*) and his efforts to show that the only valid kind of knowledge is experience. The best critical approach to this problem is to recognize, as Conrad seems to have, that the story is a traditional sea journey to knowledge and to note that in its first sentences it links the concepts of "experience" and "knowledge." Crane's first sentences extend his subtitle's emphasis on factual experience and begin systematically to identify what can be "known" with what can be "experienced.". . .

EXPERIENCE AS KNOWLEDGE

Throughout "The Open Boat," Crane uses "know" in a way that excludes the *OED*'s third sense of the word. From the first sentence to the last, he systematically denies his men the verifiable knowledge that "cognizance," "observation," or "inquiry" imply. Instead, he makes them confront what we normally think of as the unknown or the unknowable— as when they attain a "new ignorance of the grave-edge"— and leaves them only with the kind of knowledge that we refer to in such expressions as "I have known sorrow," that is, "I have felt or experienced sorrow." The story's path to this knowledge is easily traced: it begins with the curious formulation about *knowing* colors and leads the correspondent to the moment when, having *felt* nature's cold indifference to his pleas, he can come to "know" "the pathos of his situation." In bringing together "know" and "pathos" in this crucial moment, Crane underscores the meaning of "experience" in "The Open Boat": as "to know" carries the primary sense "to experience," so does "pathos," whose root extends to the Greek *paschein*, "to experience, suffer." Like Gloucester and King Lear, Crane's correspondent has come to "see feelingly." Thus, having heard "the great sea's voice" at the end of the story, he and the other survivors "*felt* that they could then be interpreters" (my emphasis).

THE CAPTAIN

Whether Crane consciously played on the etymological link between "pathos" and "experience" in "The Open Boat," it is impossible to tell. But clearly he was building toward the correspondent's moment of vision in part 6. And his next step in dramatizing the development of this religious experience was to depict in his characterization of Captain Murphy a nearly heroic figure who embodies religious values that derive directly from actual experience. Throughout the story, Crane emphasizes that the captain steadies the men with his constant calmness and serenity. Speaking of the "personal and heartfelt" quality in the captain's voice and of the men's obedience to him, Crane tells us that "after this devotion to the commander of the boat, there was this comradeship, that the correspondent, for instance, who had been taught to be cynical of men, knew even at the time was the best experience of his life." The captain will become an object of devotion, and Crane's understanding of the captain's heroism is indicated in his initial portrait. Crane sets it off from the others' portraits by placing it last, by making it longer and more detailed than the others, and by rendering it in sounded, rhythmic language:

> The injured captain, lying in the bow, was at this time buried in that profound dejection and indifference which comes, temporarily at least, to even the bravest and most enduring when, willy-nilly, the firm fails, the army loses, the ship goes down. The mind of the master of a vessel is rooted deep in the timbers of her, though he command for a day or a decade; and this captain had on him the stern impression of a scene in the grays of dawn of seven turned faces, and later a stump of a topmast with a white ball on it, that slashed to and fro at the waves, went low and lower, and down. Thereafter there was something strange in his voice. Although steady, it was deep with mourning, and of a quality beyond oration or tears.

. . . Despite his injury, or because of it, the experienced captain retains his heroic grasp of reality. He knows where he is and helps the men find their own bearings: "'See it?' said the captain," once, pointing toward the lighthouse. "'Look again. . . . It's exactly in that direction.'" Crane comments, "It took an anxious eye to find a lighthouse so tiny." And even in the whirling surf, with "his face turned away from the shore" toward his men, the captain repeatedly calls, "Come to the boat!" This selfless, experienced "iron man" to whom the men are so devoted exerts a growing influence over them that is most apparent in the "curiously iron-bound friendship, the subtle brotherhood of men" that develops among them. In a very definite sense, Captain Murphy fathers this "subtle brotherhood."

"After" the crew's "devotion" to Captain Murphy ("it was

more than a mere recognition of what was best for the common safety"), "there was this comradeship" that the correspondent sees pictured in the other men, asleep underfoot as
he rows: "The cook's arm was around the oiler's shoulders,
and, with their fragmentary clothing and haggard faces, they
were the babes of the sea." Largely because of the captain's
influence, then, the correspondent ceases his raging and
fully enters this childlike and innocent brotherhood of seamen. Gradually Crane introduces a refrain about the men's
prolonged rowing that will eventually displace the refrain of
rage: "If I am going to be drowned ... why?" He uses the
new refrain three times in parts 3 and 4, first in an extended
way: "The oiler and the correspondent rowed. And also they
rowed. They sat together in the same seat, and each rowed
an oar. Then the oiler took both oars; then the correspondent
took both oars; then the oiler; then the correspondent. They
rowed and they rowed." This refrain gives way to the simpler
refrain that appears three times in parts 5 and 6, first when
the oiler, overpowered and blinded with sleep, "rowed yet afterward": "Then he touched a man in the bottom of the boat,
and called his name. 'Will you spell me for a little while?' he
said meekly." The correspondent replies, "Sure, Billie." And
then, after his dark night alone (he "thought he was the one
man afloat on all the oceans"), he speaks into the bottom of
the boat, "Billie! ... Billie, will you spell me?" The oiler
replies, "Sure." And before their last day dawns, they change
places again in the open boat:

"Billie! ... Billie, will you spell me?"
"Sure," said the oiler.

The essential values of Crane's brotherhood are sealed in
these exchanges between Billie and the correspondent. And
yet, as Crane emphasizes in the narrative development of his
story, it is only in the intensity of his religious experience in
part 6 that the correspondent can "plainly" see and articulate the significance of what he had come to feel. His vision
of a dying "comrade" and of himself taking "that comrade's
hand" is "an actuality—stern, mournful, and fine." And
Crane explicitly articulates the change that this vision
brought about in the correspondent: he "was moved by a
profound and perfectly impersonal comprehension. He was
sorry for the soldier of the Legion who lay dying in Algiers."

Crane's short sea journey took him exactly this far: from
the condition of one "who had been taught to be cynical of

men" to that of a man who had been "moved" to feel sorrow for another. . . .

THE IMPORTANCE OF THE CORRESPONDENT'S VISION

It is a gross misreading of "The Open Boat" to deny the emotion, mystery, and sentiment in the correspondent's vision in part 6; these are natural and essential accompaniments in the epiphany or "religious experience" that William James would have recognized partly *because* of its "sentimentality" and "emotionality." Readings of the story that do not recognize the correspondent's epiphany for what it is—a newly apprehended sense of the "divine" or of "primal reality," as James would say—can grasp neither the enormous personal significance of Crane's experience nor the story's development as a traditional voyage from its initial moment when "none of them knew the colour of the sky." Such readings would suggest that Crane's brief sea journey led him not to a knowledge of "the pathos of his situation," as he said, but to the bathos.

Perhaps it is true, as James said, that "in all these matters of sentiment one must have 'been there' one's self in order to understand them." In writing "The Open Boat" Crane was certainly aware that he might be unable to reach the reader who had not "been there," whose "mind unused to the sea" could not grasp even the simple realities of the sea that he presented. As he wrote in "War Memories," "we can never *tell* life, one to another" (*Wounds in the Rain*, 229, my emphasis). But compelled, after the *Commodore* sank, to recreate the best experience of his life, he told of the intimate proximity of four men in a boat. Depicting their devotion to the captain, their shared labor, and their huddling together and touching each other for warmth, he dramatized the physical reality of the spiritual fact: "The subtle brotherhood of men . . . dwelt in the boat, and each man felt it warm him." The shocking success of his effort, as Conrad suggested, earned him a place in the brotherhood of American writers who have "been there," at sea, and honored the brotherhood of seamen they knew. This is a constant impulse in the tradition of American sea fiction, from Melville's chapter "A Squeeze of the Hand" in *Moby-Dick*, through successive scenes in Crane, Thornton Jenkins Hains, Bill Adams, Lincoln Colcord, Richard Matthews Hallet, and Hemingway. And as each of these men would know, the brotherhood's vital source is itself constant in the sea experience of any time, as one can feel it, for example, in the fisherman's story from *The Alaska Fisherman's Journal* of November 1978. Reporting how the fishing vessel *Marion A* sank in Geese Channel off Kodiak Island, the *Journal* quoted the lone survivor. His friend Jerry helped him disentangle and climb into the single survival suit that floated to the surface after the *Marion A* went down. The captain had already disappeared. Then:

"I told Jerry to hold around my waist. He kicked while I kicked and swam. I told him to keep kicking.

"We were closer to the island side and I wanted to go that way but the wind was blowing us (in the opposite direction). Every time I tried to turn into it, Jerry would say, 'Just go with the tide, go with the wind.'

"Well, he only said it a couple times. . . . Jerry slowed down. Started talking real slow. He knew it and I knew it: It was going to take too long to hit land.

"He said, 'I love you, Joe.' I said, 'I love you, too.' He kissed me on the cheek and I kissed him on the cheek. I said, 'We're going to make this. Just keep kicking. Open your eyes.' I held him until he collapsed in my arms and then I held him longer. I was sure he was dead. I finally let go."

"The Open Boat" Is a Story of Revelation

Frank Bergon

Critic Frank Bergon is the author of *Stephen Crane's Artistry* and a member of the English Department at Vassar College. In the following article, Bergon critiques "The Open Boat," praising its realism. Bergon believes the characters in the story progress from ignorance to a keen awareness of nature and of themselves.

In "The Open Boat," Crane fixes his attention so closely on immediate experience that the story becomes a step-by-step process of acquiring "new eyes." Everything extraneous to this main concern is eliminated, the question of heroism is not even asked, and Crane moves relentlessly toward un-buffered contact with the realities of existence. "The Open Boat" is then not so much a story of learning as of realiza-tion. Certainly the correspondent, who had been taught to be the most cynical of men, knows that nature is indifferent, but hours on the sea cause him to experience this truth with re-newed intensity. Though it may be assumed that a growth in awareness affects moral intelligence, the "long logic" of the story is based on a psychological rather than a moral pro-gression. Constant contact with the wind and waves affects, before anything else, the men's senses and perceptions. Gradually, as these unfamiliar circumstances become famil-iar, natural responses of anger and self-pity give way to gen-eral pity and, finally, to no emotion at all. Anxiety reaches its peak when man's mental processes are most active but fa-tigue soon drives out rage: the correspondent's mind "was dominated *at this time* by the muscles, and the muscles said they did not care. It merely occurred to him that if he should drown it would be a shame" (emphasis added).

It is the correspondent, the man of words, who discovers

that questions based on preconceptions of an event in no way anticipate the questions asked when that event becomes reality. Formulations do not control or explain experience. It is reality itself, the actual immersion in the cold sea, that formulates the surprisingly limited and puzzled realizations of a man in touch with the great death. "I am going to drown? Can it be possible? Can it be possible? Can it be possible?" The correspondent comes as close as is humanly possible to approximating a cosmic point of view when he is both involved in his experience and detached from it. Like Fleming's insights [in *The Red Badge of Courage*], each of the correspondent's realizations is momentary, occurring only at that time, but unlike Fleming's experience, these series of moments form a progression. That progression may not be truer to life than are Henry's vacillations and regressions, but they do make for a tighter, more compact story and a more decisive impact.

VARIED POINTS OF VIEW

An experience of riding the edge of death is such a mysterious thing that it cannot be reduced to a single meaning. To say only that the men learn of nature's indifference and of their own bonds of brotherhood is to diminish that experience. Multiple points of view are needed to perceive this strange event. The views range from immediate, limited perception—"Far ahead, where coastline, sea, and sky formed their mighty angle, there were little dots which seemed to indicate a city on the shore"—to authorial omniscience: "It is fair to say here that there was not a life-saving station within twenty miles in either direction; but the men did not know this fact...." This last remark both provides information and accentuates the point of the dialogue preceding it, the inherent impulse of the human mind to play tricks on itself. Another voice in "The Open Boat" narrates how this experience might perhaps be seen when "Viewed from a balcony." It is a cautious voice, stating only that the men's "eyes must have glinted in strange ways as they gazed steadily astern." The voice often uses a vocabulary (not out of reach of the correspondent) based upon a distant and often sentimental view of such an experience: "It was probably splendid...." It is often the voice of a man safe on the shore jocosely narrating the story: "By the very last star of truth, it is easier to steal eggs from under a hen that it was to change seats in the dingey." These statements serve to remind the reader of an attitude informing the entire narrative; indeed, "Shipwrecks are *apropos* of nothing."

At the same time, in their sentiment and point of view, such statements contrast keenly with the concerns and experience of the men in the boat. They do not contradict the men's experience, but they emphasize its seriousness and intensity. These often light, pithy remarks also give the story some emotional modulation that is not mere contrivance, for despite preconceptions that such an experience at sea is always one of terror, the mood of these statements does not clash with those brief moments in the open boat when tension abates and the men feel a certain "lightheartedness." Also, the voice reflects an emotional detachment which the correspondent himself eventually achieves during the final moments of the story, when he supposedly apprehends his situation properly.

COMPARISONS WITH EVERYDAY OBJECTS

Since the profundity of the men's experience eludes definition, it often can only be measured by reference to what may be considered normal. A series of commonplace objects drawn from life on land—a bathtub, slate, mats, canton-flannel, carpets, prairie chickens, ham sandwiches, a jackknife, eggs, paper, pie, cigars, furniture, tea, a couch, a mattress, a broad fence—are used to help describe this experience. But just as the wind and waves eventually frustrate all attempts to make sense of the situation from a normal, ego-centered point of view, these objects gradually accentuate the gulf between commonplace experience and this grim exposure to sea and sky. By its very nature, this moment on the sea separates elements of experience that are more complexly bound together on land. Both death and life are part of experience on the shore, but on land the reality of death is obscured by social intercourse and human bonds. Its terror is diminished, and man need not constantly face his own limitations. On the sea, only six inches of gunwale separate potential death from a communal existence which is almost a parody of that on land. The men puff big cigars, the cook asks the oiler, "what kind of pie do you like best?" and the correspondent muses about what the experience has taught him and grows to understand "that if he were given another opportunity he would mend his conduct

and his words, and be better and brighter during an introduction, or at tea." These actions, words, and thoughts perform two immediate functions: they underscore man's puny
position in contrast to the void around him, and they seem
to mock those trite pleasures and formalities that dominate
life on the shore.

The breakdown of life into the elemental and the trivial
performs yet another function: the incongruous juxtaposition creates the story's essential drama, for though the story
is certainly about the great death, it is also as much about
life. One of the more suggestive remarks about "The Open
Boat" is Berryman's comment that "the death is so close that
the story is warm." The physical coldness of sea and air, in
contrast, makes the cook "almost stove-like" after he "had
tied a life-belt around himself in order to get even the
warmth which this clumsy cork contrivance could donate."
In contrast to the sea, the cold water in the boat is actually
"comfortable" when a man settles into it, "huddled close to
the cook's life-belt"; and a rower finds that he can "keep his
feet partly warm by thrusting them under his companions."
There is also "the subtle brotherhood of men ... and each
man felt it warm him." Simple, trivial pleasures and courte-
sies glow with astonishing warmth. When juxtaposed
against cold nothingness, rituals of serving tea or sharing a
cigar with friends become things of importance, goods in
themselves. If nothing else, they give evidence of life and
create human bonds. Only a man who has faced the cruelty
and ignorance of the grave, Crane seems to say, can know
the true importance of being warm, tender, and kind, even at
tea or during an introduction.

A REALISTIC INTERPRETATION

To render the actuality of life in an open boat Crane relied
on all the sensory and suggestive means that identify his
writing at its best. The rowers do not grow tired, but the oars
become "leaden"; the men do not move toward land, but
"brown mats of seaweed that appeared from time to time ...
informed the men in the boat that it was making progress
slowly toward the land." The meaning of "The Open Boat" is
the sum of all its details. Yet such details do not make a story.
No matter how realistic, a description of four men danger-
ously adrift on an open sea is still an episode. Without resort
to a traditional plot or conflict between characters, Crane

nevertheless instilled this fragment of experience, and many others, with the formal authority of a complete statement. Natural patterns, not *necessarily* dependent on plot development, satisfy man's craving to close every broken circle, to complete every truncated rhythm. For example, the first three chapters of *Maggie* produce an illusion of wholeness not because there is a resolution of conflicting action or emotion but because there is a cyclical completion of natural processes. Events begin in the day, continue into the night, and come to a close with the breaking of dawn. It is a mistake to overlook the formal simplicity of "The Open Boat," for the very simplicity of its organization makes it a more strongly ordered story than if it had been given a carefully contrived plot.

"THE OPEN BOAT" IS CRANE'S GREATEST WORK

Though "The Open Boat" is of a piece with Crane's major fiction, it stands apart from other works in style, characterization, and tone. In Crane's handling of these elements we see finally fulfilled the potential indicated so many times in his other publications. Only once did Crane fully realize that potential, "The Open Boat" being the high point of his brief career. The fluency of style here, its evenness throughout, gives evidence, especially when compared with the style of Crane's other good pieces, of his having a clear and exact notion of what he was about in executing "The Open Boat." Very few of those infelicitous phrases and inept comparisons occurring in nearly all of Crane's work appear here. One reason they do not occur is that his feelings toward his characters are settled as well as are his feelings about the total situation. He does not find it necessary to retreat from these characters by treating them ironically, thus turning them into objects, into beings whose humanity he does not grant. This implies a consistency of tone nearly unparalleled in Crane's major fiction.

Donald B. Gibson, *The Fiction of Stephen Crane*. Carbondale: Southern Illinois University Press, 1968.

It has always been natural for man to imagine life as a journey, even if the goal of that journey is a biological inevitability. Both things happen at the end of "The Open Boat"; the men reach the real goal of their journey, the comfort of land, and one of the men reaches that end of which any completed journey can be a symbol. The triumph of "The Open Boat" is that form and theme are one. While the men are on the sea, life and death are fragilely separated by a few inches of gunwale; the men settle into the "cold comfortable sea-water" within the boat, but the correspondent jerks his hand away from the "tumbling, boiling flood of white water" that splashes up from the sea. There are simulations of human comfort in the boat, and there are promises of death from the sea. Comfort is cold while potential death is boiling. Back on the land, order is restored. The comfort that was parodied and the death that was threatened simultaneously became actualities, and the tenuous separation between the two evaporates: at the same time that the "welcome of the land" is "warm and generous" with real blankets, clothes, flasks, and coffee pots, its welcome also consists of "the different and sinister hospitality of the grave."

A SCHOOLBOY INDIFFERENCE

Reinforcing this simple design is a sequence of events that occur according to a strict but cyclical chronology, beginning with one dawn and drawing to a close with another. Little need be said about the relation of this natural process to the expansion of perception that constitutes most of the narrative "action." Absorbed by the demands of their situation, the men experience a restricted vision, and the first "process of the breaking day was unknown to them"; but after they grow accustomed to life in the boat and less stunned by nature's insult to themselves as individuals, they can begin to direct attention away from themselves and the problems of navigation. As the unfamiliar grows familiar, they are able to look around, and the next dawn is seen both on the water and in the sky. The self-absorbed, questioning, and even raging correspondent becomes a calm, depersonalized observer. His new eyes are more extreme than Fleming's, for he does not even bother to acknowledge that everything is explained to him except why he himself is there. Events have forced him to see with detachment. After a man has been continuously beaten by sea and wind, he becomes a different thing. All the things that once seemed so important to the correspondent now no longer mean that much to him, including his own fate. Not even the actual experience of tumbling into the surf is as he expected, for the "January water was icy, and he reflected immediately that it was

colder than he had expected to find it off the coast of Florida.
This appeared to his dazed mind as a fact important enough
to be noted *at the time*" (emphasis added). No doubt upon
later reflection, the correspondent would be surprised at his
detachment: the coastline "was very near to him then, but he
was impressed as one who in a gallery looks at a scene from
Brittany or Holland." Ironically, the correspondent has
moved from a state in which he felt such poignancy in the
fate of a legendary soldier to one that is nearer to his former
schoolboy indifference. Perhaps that soldier's feeling was
comparable to his own now that he was tossing about in the
water: "when one gets properly wearied, drowning must really be a comfortable arrangement, a cessation of hostilities
accompanied by a large degree of relief." This attitude was
foreshadowed when, in the boat, the mere passage of time
and the increase of fatigue allowed the men to accept their
circumstances, to sleep and, as the correspondent does, to
look at a shark with the calm, unexcited vision of a veteran.
To emphasize the contrast between preconceptions and experience, Crane states discursively, "The presence of this
biding thing did not affect the man with the same horror that
it would if he had been a picnicker. He simply looked at the
sea dully and swore in an undertone."

THE EXPERIENCE OF THE CORRESPONDENT

When the correspondent is finally flung into the icy water,
the reflections, patterns, designs, and poetic sentiments that
give point to experience are of little worth. He sees for the
first time with his own eyes and trusts his senses. He mar-
vels at things that would never enter the mind of a picnicker
who might happen to reflect on the possibility of drowning
at sea. His past life does not stream through his mind, he
makes no resolutions to mend his ways, he does not ask why
he is there, and he is not overcome by frantic impulses to
reach safety. "There is a certain immovable quality to a
shore, and the correspondent wondered at it amid the confusion of the sea. It seemed also very attractive, . . . and he
paddled leisurely." He does not panic or rage when he has
"arrived at a place in the sea where travel was beset with difficulty. He did not pause swimming to inquire what manner
of current caught him, but there his progress ceased." He
sees the shore in its detail, and noticing the captain grasping
the leaping boat with one hand, he "marveled that the cap-

tain could still hold to it." After awhile, still unable to advance, he does wonder simply, "I am going to drown? Can it be possible? . . . But later a wave perhaps whirled him out of this small deadly current, for he found suddenly that he could again make progress toward the shore."

Amid this limited, uninterpretive rendition of the correspondent's sensations, perceptions, and thoughts, another voice intrudes, that jocular voice of a man safe on shore. A large wave catches the correspondent and flings him safely over the boat and far from harm. This event strikes the correspondent as "an event in gymnastics, and a true miracle of the sea." That other voice adopts a different, ego-dominated point of view and comments that in being tossed by the wave, "the correspondent performed his one little marvel of the voyage." Is this how the correspondent will at times look back on this occurrence when his faculties and his vanity return to him?

After he and his companions have reached the shore safely, when night has fallen and they are probably warming themselves by a fire, "they felt that they could then be interpreters." The statement is cautious; there is no guarantee that they actually can interpret the experience they have had, but they *feel* they can; and that feeling comes only "then," when they are out of the waves. Any discursive statement they might make or any reflection they might have will necessarily be partial and reductive. Crane makes no attempt to sum up this experience, for the total meaning and proper interpretation resides in the "form and color" of the experience itself, for which one must return to the beginning of the story. To conceptualize any more, or to write a newspaper account, would be a false interpretation. As an artifact, "The Open Boat" is already an interpretation, but it is so close a paradigm of the experience itself that anything more would be a distortion. . . .

CRANE AS A SHORT STORY WRITER

Since Crane's time, readers faced with stories having virtually no plot or conventional action have managed to discover a shift in focal point from the ending to some epiphany or nuance of character within the story. This epiphany may be shared by the character, or it may not, in which case a mask is stripped from the character for the reader's benefit. The form of many of Crane's stories does duplicate this process of growing awareness, and a character's relation to it is often a major motif; but a reading which narrowly interprets stories solely in these terms does not suit Crane's work as well as it might that of Chekhov, Joyce, Mansfield, or even James. First, there are too many other points of view in Crane's fiction, and his characters' insights are usually partial and momentary. Second, in a sense there are no characters in his work, or their importance as individuals is diminished. If plot might be said to issue from interactions between characters, then the sea is as important a character in "The Open Boat" as any of the men. Some of this diminishment of character may be attributed to the genre itself; the short story simply does not allow for characterization as does a novel. One or two evocative details must suffice. The description of Scratchy Wilson's shirt and red-topped boots "with gilded imprints, of the kind beloved in winter by little sledding boys on the hillsides of New England" replaces any number of events which might deflate the character's authenticity as a gunslinger. It might be argued that any fictional character is only a name and a series of words describing gestures and sounds, but it must be admitted that Crane's use of such words is severely restricted. He is even reluctant to name his characters. This apparent lack of interest in creating anything more than a "type" reconfirms the short story as the best genre for this peculiar impetus of Crane's imagination. . . .

THE JUMBLE OF FEELING

Crane's characters are nameless, fragmented, depersonalized, and passive because his attention is usually on that jumble of feeling and sensation that constitutes immediate experience and precedes any sense of self. This is man's normal state; extreme situations only intensify it. Thus momentary states of being and consciousness become more important than action in Crane's characterizations. A man is defined by what he feels. Emotions become characters and syntactically assume positions in sentences as agents of action; but emotional states are more complex than language suggests, and Crane demonstrates this complexity by rendering a large number of discordant but simultaneous sensations and emotions. Even the simplest gesture may be the product of frothing, contradictory feelings: "Then the captain, in the bow, chuckled in a way that expressed humor, contempt, tragedy, all in one."

The effect that feelings have on personality is most extreme when some intense emotion, particularly rage, forces its way to awareness. How a man sees reveals his state of being. Under intense emotion, the world falls away, a man loses perspective on his relation to what is around him; but a similar state of depersonalization also occurs when a man is most aware, when the world is seen in keenest perspective, when a man becomes most completely and perfectly himself. At these moments of sensitive attunement, the characters see with a fullness and clarity that the reader is meant to share when he, too, apprehends the details as well as the quality of a scene. All Crane's techniques of style, form, and characterization can bring a scene or situation to such a still point. Revealed then are the form and color of an incident. The quality evoked by these revelations—what Coleridge called that "continuous under-current of feeling...everywhere present"— once again defines Crane's visionary habit of seeing the world as simultaneously ominous and splendid.

Crane's Lapses of Style in "The Open Boat" Are Purposeful

Donna Gerstenberger

Donna Gerstenberger is a professor of English at the
University of Washington and the author of several
critical works, including a book on Irish playwright
John Synge. In the following article, Gerstenberger
insists that the lapses in style and vocabulary found
in "The Open Boat" and so frequently pointed out by
critics of Crane's work are purposeful and instructive. Crane means to jar the reader into noticing his
ironic touches, and to probe the story's characters
and their failure to learn from their journey.

Stephen Crane's "The Open Boat" is generally acknowledged to be among the masterpieces of the modern short
story. The question of the story's excellence has never been
debated; the only questions have been the proper means of
defining the story's modernity and of accounting for what
appear to be certain awkwardnesses of style, tone, and point
of view.

"The Open Boat" has been hailed as an example of naturalistic fiction at its best until recent years, when the auto-
matic and somewhat naive tendency to equate naturalism
and modernity has been called into question in all the arts.
Thus Peter Buitenhuis asserts in a recent study, "'The Open
Boat' is not a naturalistic story," and he confronts the story
as "existentialist fiction," concentrating on Crane's ironic
presentation and the story's demonstration of the absurdity
of the human condition. While Mr. Buitenhuis does not ad-
dress himself to the question of "The Open Boat" as a *modern* short story, the implicit assumption is that use of the
term *existential* automatically confers the status of modernity, as well it may. Yet such a reading leaves its author trou-

Excerpted from Donna Gerstenberger, "'The Open Boat': An Additional Perspective,"
Modern Fiction Studies, Winter 1971–72, pp. 557–61; ©1971 The Johns Hopkins University Press. Reprinted with permission of the publisher.

bled by the same kinds of questions that troubled those who saw the story as naturalistic fiction—questions about Crane's style and about the story's protagonist. The answers to such questions come into focus when "The Open Boat" is viewed as a story with an emphasis on the epistemological aspect of the existential crisis.

The epistemological question about the problems of knowing and the limitations of man's ability to see and to know has become both subject and style in modern art from Conrad to Joyce, Picasso to Faulkner, Pirandello to Beckett. So persistent and pervasive has been the preoccupation with epistemological questions in modern art that it might almost be said to constitute a way of defining one aspect of modernity. Conversely, it might be said that the somewhat naive and programmatic view of reality held by the naturalists gives their work a certain old-fashioned quality, which Crane's story, demonstrably, does not share. "The Open Boat" calls equally into question the assumptions of photographic reality as well as those of idealized, romantic views of the universe.

With his opening sentence, "None of them knew the colour of the sky," Crane makes clear a major concern of "The Open Boat." The word *knew* in this famous first sentence is the key word, for the story which follows is about man's limited capacities for knowing reality. This opening sentence leads the reader toward the concluding line of the story, ". . . and the wind brought the sound of the great sea's voice to the men on the shore, and they felt that they could then be interpreters"—a conclusion which, when the special emphasis of the story is acknowledged, is a good deal more complex than has generally been thought.

HUMANITY'S VISION ALWAYS FLAWED

Crane's irony in "The Open Boat" grows out of the epistemological direction of the story. It is invested in the language and in the authorial point of view as well as in tone. This irony, based on Crane's perception of the disparity between man's vision of a just and meaningful universe and a world totally indifferent to such unrealistic notions, acknowledges the absurdity at the heart of the existentialist vision. Yet Crane, through his ironic treatment of his material, moves one step further: the implication of "The Open Boat" is that the vision of any human being must, of necessity, be false, *even if* that vision be a knowledge of the absurdity of the universe.

This extension of the epistemological question makes it clear that Crane intentionally divides his points of view among the various characters, and it is difficult to accept Peter Buitenhuis's conclusion that

> Unfortunately, instead of confining these attitudes to a single character, the protagonist, Crane shifts at times to the points of view of the oiler, the cook, and the captain as well. He was probably trying to emphasize through this device that the experience was deeply shared by the four men, a point essential to the story's conclusion. However, in attributing to the four not only similar emotions but also similar formulations about the nature of existence, he presumes too much on the reader's willing suspension of disbelief. Crane also unnecessarily seeks to make his point by using the omniscient point of view.

To conclude, as Buitenhuis has, that Crane is mistaken in his failure to present his story from a single point of view, is to assert that Crane intended his story to be something other than it is, to assume that the sole aim of the story is a demonstration of the absurdity of the universe. I would suggest, on the contrary, that while the shared experience of absurdity is an aspect of the story, Crane's intention includes a demonstration of the impossibility of knowing anything with objective certainty, given the subjective, human instrument for perception.

The kind of authorial intrusion represented by the famous passage, "Viewed from a balcony, the whole thing would doubtless have been weirdly picturesque," can be accepted within the framework of Crane's intention when it is understood that, although the man on the balcony would have a distancing perspective not available to the men in the boat, he would be wrong about what he would be seeing. The human need to translate the open boat into the landscape terms of "picturesque" immediately falsifies at the same time that it represents a truth of human perception. The reader is reminded once again, by a passage like this, that a part of the injustice, the absurdity of the universe, is man's inability ever to know anything about the complex whole of experience.

In a similar kind of response, the correspondent, looking shoreward, contemplates the tall white windmill amidst the deserted cottages, which, in an echo of Goldsmith's formalized landscape, "might have formed a deserted village" and picturesquely sees it as "a giant, standing with its back to the plight of the ants." To see the wind tower is to translate it into something else, into a reality invested with subjective meaning, even though that meaning be a statement about the objectivity of nature. For the tower "represented in a degree, to the correspondent, the serenity of nature amid the struggles of the individual—nature in the wind, and nature in the vision of man."

PERSISTENT IGNORANCE

In much of modern literature, there is a sense in which existential man sometimes seems to achieve a modicum of heroic stature when he apprehends and accepts the absurd universe, for he has done what man can do, and insofar as he has done what all men are not able to do, he stands apart from the common run of men. Crane, however, is not willing to grant to his correspondent an heroic moment as a result of the "right" kind of perception (which in itself, in existential terms, often becomes a kind of absolute), for as the correspondent contemplates the flat indifference of nature, "a distinction between right and wrong seems absurdly clear to him, then, in this new ignorance of the grave-edge, and he understands that if he were given another opportunity he would mend his conduct and his words, and be better and brighter during an introduction or at tea."

One might expect Crane to speak of the man's "new *knowledge* of the grave-edge," but his insistence upon *ignorance* denies the correspondent the absolute sanction so often bestowed as a result of confronting hard reality. Further, the conclusion of the passage, "he would mend his conduct and his words, and be better and brighter during an introduction or at a tea" has the same kind of anti-heroic effect worked so neatly upon T.S. Eliot's Prufrock, who can hardly be expected to force any moment to its crisis within the context of "tea and cakes and ices." Crane refuses to permit his reader comfort of the kind involved in the equation that when the man who suffers becomes the man who *knows,* something of absolute value, however depressing, has been achieved.

Crane's practice of using apparently inappropriate or consciously awkward metaphors, analogies, or descriptive adjectives, which appear to devalue or overvalue in specific passages, challenges the reader's too-easy assumptions about what may be defined as heroic within the context of experiential stress. Several examples from the opening pages of the story may suggest the achievement of this general technique: "By the very last star of truth, it is easier to steal eggs from under a hen than it was to change seats in the dinghy." The linking of absolute abstraction ("the very last star of truth") with the homely, agrarian observation about the difficulty of stealing eggs from under a hen seems as inappropriate to the act of changing rowers as do the parts to each other. But the purpose of heroic deflation, of irony, is served, as it is in the serviceable awkwardness of the following: "In a ten-foot dinghy one can get an idea of the resources of the sea in the line of waves that is not probable to the average experience, which is never at sea in a dinghy." Crane refuses to romanticize the absurdity of experience, and the reader is constantly reminded that experience, like perception, is betrayed by the language by which it is conceptualized.

Not only does Crane constantly deny by stylistic devices the heroism of action or even of enduring necessity, but he also denies the heroism of knowledge in the context discussed above. Crane's extensive use of the subjunctive mood is a part of his statement that even a tough-minded view of the universe involves man in an uncertain questioning of the conditions within which his responses, even to absurdity, must be framed.

FALSE PERCEPTIONS

Examples of this kind all bear on the claim that "The Open Boat" may best be viewed as a story with an epistemological emphasis, one which constantly reminds its reader of the impossibility of man's *knowing* anything, even that which he experiences. The reaction of the correspondent, near the close of the story, to his fight for life against a hostile current is of interest because of its reminders of earlier passages central to an understanding of the story. He sees the shore, the white beach, and "green bluff topped with little silent cottages . . . spread like a picture before him." The shore, in fact, is very close at this point, but "he was impressed as one who, in a gallery, looks at a scene from Brittany or Algiers." The immanence of death, the difficulty of achieving the shore, formalizes experience once again into landscape, reminding the reader of the necessarily false perception of the earlier hypothetical view of the open boat from a balcony. (The use of the word *gallery*, a term also meaning *balcony*, reinforces the relationship of the two passages.) The locating of the landscape in "Brittany or Algiers" inevitably calls up a vision of the soldier of the Legion dying in Algiers, both in the romanticized picture of Lady Carolyn Bingen's lines and also in terms of the moment of understanding and fellow feeling that the correspondent experiences as he pictures the soldier lying "on the sand with his feet out straight and still." "It was no longer merely a picture of a few throes in the breast of a poet, meanwhile drinking tea and warming his feet at the grate; it was an actuality—stern, mournful, and fine."

It has generally been assumed that the soldier dying in Algiers is important to Crane's intentions in "The Open Boat" because he provides the opportunity for a clear example of the kind of understanding, of human sympathy, of the valuable kind of knowledge which comes from experiential stress. In this respect, "The Open Boat" has been viewed as an "initiation" story, pre-figuring Hemingway's use of experiential stress as a key to knowledge. But it is important to bear in mind that the correspondent's new attitude toward the soldier falsifies, as do all the "pictures" or "landscapes" by which man seeks a delineated context for knowledge. The story in its totality makes it perfectly clear (as do Crane's other tales) that there is nothing "stern, mournful, and fine" in death, and this incident, which has generally been read as indicative of the correspondent's growth in knowing, may well serve as an example of the impossibility of untainted knowledge. To *know* the soldier in Algiers without a self-pitying desire to find something "stern, mournful, and fine" in death is not possible. The death of Billie, the oiler, contrasts with the picture of the soldier's death, and it certainly is indicative of the indifference of nature, for the arbitrary absurdity of his death is underlined by the fact that he is the strongest and the most realistic of the men aboard the dinghy. Crane's description of his death is presented more starkly than anything else in the story: "In the shallows, face downward lay the oiler. His forehead touched sand that was periodically, between each wave, clear of the sea." No pictures, no objectifying landscapes, no stylistic ironies. The question of human perception is no longer a problem that applies to the oiler.

Within the epistemological context discussed in this paper, it would seem necessary, finally, to raise a question about the concluding lines of Crane's story: "the wind brought the sound of the great sea's voice to the men on the shore, and they felt that they could then be interpreters." The story has clearly shown the final absurdity to be the falsification of man's attempts to "interpret," an act in which he is betrayed by the very language he must use to conceptualize, by the narrowness of vision, and by the further limitation of his need to frame, to formalize his apprehensions in a landscape, a poem, an irony, or a subjunctive statement of conditions that never were on land or sea. To "interpret" is not to be equated with knowing, and perhaps the final irony is in the community of shared experience which these final lines seem to suggest, for however communal the interpretation of the "great sea's voice," nothing in the story suggests that any one of the three men remaining can conceptualize the death of the oiler without, perhaps, falsely transfiguring him into a figure like the soldier of the Legion, whose death was "an actuality—stern, mournful, and fine."

CHAPTER 4

Other Works

READINGS ON

STEPHEN CRANE

Maggie: *A Girl of the Streets* Portrays a "Survival of the Fittest" World

David Fitelson

In the following article, critic David Fitelson argues that the characters in *Maggie* represent a Darwinian struggle. Biologist Charles Darwin's theory of evolution predicts the survival of the strongest and/or most cunning. Fitelson interprets Crane as saying that because Maggie is not strong enough, or ruthless enough, to live in her amoral world, she commits suicide.

Possibly the most arresting critical problem posed by Stephen Crane's first novel is that of the disposition of mind that lies behind and shapes it—the ideology, so to speak, that it communicates. The problem is especially arresting because this ideology has never been closely defined, although it is often alluded to as comprising Crane's early Naturalism. Of his ideological intentions in the novel, Crane himself has been gnomic. He observed on one occasion that "I had no other purpose in writing 'Maggie' than to show people to people as they seem to me," and on another that "[the purpose was] to show that environment is a tremendous thing in this world, and often shapes lives regardless." The statements, I should think, are contradictory. Taken together, they are scarcely helpful. . . .

Luckily, *Maggie*, unlike most of the critical commentary engendered in its wake, provides considerable specific and reliable information about its ideology. In reading the novel, one discovers that Crane is presenting characters whose lives are rigidly circumscribed by what appear to be inexorable laws. These are unenchanted lives. Their fundamen-

Excerpted from David Fitelson, "Stephen Crane's *Maggie* and Darwinism," *American Quarterly*, vol. 16 (Summer 1964), pp. 182–94; ©1964 The Johns Hopkins University Press. Reprinted with permission of the publisher.

tal condition is violence, and this fact seems to be neither haphazard nor peculiar, but reasonable and inevitable—a condition which must necessarily prevail because the world is *governed* by violence.

A world so governed provides certain clear guidelines for the way life is to be lived within it. To the degree that a character is aware of the nature of the world, and more particularly, to the degree that he conducts his life in accordance with that nature—to that degree will he be a survivor of violence and free from frustration. Moreover, since there are no meaningful alternatives to a life of violence, conventional notions of morality are without application. The world of the novel provides no distinction between right and wrong action—except insofar as right action is that which insures survival. Survival *is*, in effect, the way of morality, and therefore the plight of the heroine, Maggie herself, who is less violent than the others and unable to compete successfully for survival, is no occasion for sympathy. It is merely an instance of self-destruction and failure.

Clearly, if all this is so, the world of this novel resembles nothing so much as the world of the jungle, and the pattern described by the lives of its characters is that of a primordial struggle for existence. Clearly, too, the law which chiefly governs this world is the law of the survival of the fittest. Now to recite, in this fashion, some of the more shopworn and tiresome rallying cries of "evolutionism" is to come substantially within reach of a definition of the novel's ideology, for that ideology clearly corresponds to some form of evolutionary doctrine. But what is not yet clear, and what the balance of this paper will attempt to demonstrate, is that the disposition of mind that shapes the novel is closely allied with certain distinctive features of the Darwinian Idea....

HUMANS AS ANIMALS

In the novel, as I shall attempt to show, Crane is not so much extending Darwin's notions of animal behavior to human society as he is reducing the conduct of human beings to the level of animal behavior.

As a novelist, Crane displays many of the techniques of a dramatist. In *Maggie* he is fundamentally an unfolder and manipulator of action. As an unfolder, he is rather conventionally the dramatist. The novel's organization is consistently scenic. Nothing that happens to the characters is unknown to the reader, who, positioned, as it were, across the footlights, has the entire breadth of the proscenium opening for a "fine central intelligence." It is as a manipulator that Crane is unique, and as a manipulator his principal technique is irony.

The unfolding of the drama, by means of description, statement and action, successfully conveys the novel's meaning—gets the point across. But it is the additional element of irony which gets it across in the particular manner that gives it its special force and which makes the reader constantly aware that a point is being made. The tale is told objectively. Crane is always an unfolder and a manipulator simultaneously, and it is this unity of method that finally insures that *Maggie is* a novel and not a thinly disguised Darwinistic tract.

To be specific, it is self-evident within the novel that violence is the predominant form of human communication. Maggie wounds her baby brother; her elder brother, Jimmie, wounds Maggie; Jimmie is wounded by their mother and father, who wound Maggie and battle with each other. Jimmie kicks his father, pummels his mother, fights with Maggie's seducer, Pete, who of course fights back. In the intervals of nonviolence nearly all of the major characters either boast of past battles or threaten new ones. As revealed dramatically this situation vividly conveys that here indeed is a jungle-like world. What informs the reader, however, that he is observing behavior not at all to be looked upon as exceptional—and on that account not at all to be condemned—is irony. If we look at the example of fighting, we see, as various characters from time to time point out, that this is not always a desirable activity. But why not? Certainly not for any "moral" reason. On one occasion Maggie complains, "Youse allus fightin', Jimmie, an' yeh knows it puts mudder out when yehs come home half dead, an' it's like we'll all get a poundin'." Another time, the father remonstrates with the mother: "When I come home nights I can't get no rest 'cause yer allus poundin' a kid." Later, the mother expresses herself to the father: "Why deh blazes don' cher try teh keep Jim from fightin'?" The father barks back: "Ah w'at's bitin' yeh...." And the mother replies: "Because he tears 'is clothes yeh fool!" In each instance the reader is informed by means of irony that fighting is undesirable because it is inappropriate in some way to the demands of the speaker's survival.

Irony is employed in similar fashion and with particular effectiveness as a means of commenting on the relationship between Maggie and her mother, a relationship which displays Crane's concern to reduce human conduct to the animal level. Specifically, it is evident from the action that the monstrous harridan, Mary, is the sort of mother whose counterpart in the animal world eats her young: but once more irony is introduced to point out that her behavior is perfectly acceptable and entirely consistent with established "morality." Upon learning that Maggie has "gone teh d' devil," her mother, who has driven her into the streets, whispers to Jimmie: "Ah, who would t'ink such a bad girl could grow up in our fambly. . . . An' after all her bringin'-up an' what I tol her and talked wid her . . .". And on Maggie's death we are confronted with the profound irony of the novel's final words, as this same mother screams in saintly judgment: "Oh, yes, I'll fergive her! I'll fergive her!"

In addition to such passages as these, in which the irony is woven into the fabric of the unfolding drama, there are numerous occasions on which Crane injects isolated statements, images and actions which serve to reinforce one's conviction that the unseemly events being narrated are actually quite in keeping with the "morality" of the novel. An example may be found in the relentlessly objective turn taken by the narrative in treating of death and the continuity of the life surrounding it. In such passages as the two following there is almost the quality of natural history:

> The babe, Tommie, died. He went away in an insignificant coffin, his small waxen hand clutching a flower that the girl, Maggie, had stolen from an Italian.
> She and Jimmie lived.
> . . . .
> So, eventually he [Jimmie] felt obliged to work. His father died, and his mother's years were divided into periods of thirty days.
> He became a truck-driver.

ANIMAL ALLUSIONS

Another example is found in the rather loose pattern of animal associations which Crane uses to relate the world of *Maggie* to the lower levels of the struggle for existence. A few specific instances: Jimmie, when first encountered, is described as "fighting in the modes of four thousands years ago" (depending, of course, on geography, this need not *nec-*

essarily be construed as an animal association). The young Maggie "ate like a small pursued tigress." The neighbors comment on the battle between father and mother: "Ol' Johnson's playin' horse agin." Pete admires a particularly belligerent monkey in a menagerie: "Ever after Pete knew that monkey by sight, and winked at him...". There is also a possible botanical association: "The girl, Maggie, blossomed in a mud-puddle. She grew to be a most rare and wonderful production of a tenement district, a pretty girl." While this last may appear promising for Maggie, her situation is somewhat analogous to that of a plant on the edge of a desert, for whom as Darwin among others has suggested, survival is problematic at best. Finally, it scarcely need be emphasized that the persistent, reciprocal warfare among members of the family is more evocative of life in the animal kingdom than it is of the world of civilized man.

The degree to which life in the novel conforms to a pattern of violence which upholds survival as the only absolute value is astonishing. In *The Origin of Species,* Darwin, generalizing on the entire animal kingdom, writes: "as more individuals are produced than can possibly survive, there must in every case be a struggle for existence, either one individual with another of the same species, or with individuals of distinct species, or with the physical conditions of life." This proposition, in each of its particulars, is attested to by the lives of the characters in *Maggie.* The baby, Tommie, is a completely helpless creature, quite unable even to begin the struggle. He is weeded out in infancy. Of the phenomenon illustrated by his death, Darwin writes: "heavy destruction inevitably falls either on the young or old, during each generation or at recurrent intervals," and: "Eggs or very young animals seem generally to suffer most." The death of Maggie's father is the palpable result of his defeat in a most particular struggle with a member of his own species, his wife: "In the quarrel between husband and wife the woman was victor." It is the result also of a more generalized struggle (in which all of the characters participate, as residents of "a tenement district") with the physical conditions of life.

MAGGIE'S MOTHER

The life of Maggie's mother is the perpetual struggle of a middle-class jungle denizen, an animal not to be ranked among the fittest, but capable of swallowing many others be-

fore being swallowed itself, and with a nerve-racking ability
to stay just out of reach of the fitter beasts. She survives in
part by virtue of what Darwin has helpfully called "diversity,"
the ability to adopt "variations" which "from whatever cause
proceeding, if they be in any degree profitable to the individuals of a species, in their infinitely complex relations to other
organic beings and to their physical conditions of life, will
tend to the preservation of such individuals." Her ironically
portrayed capacity for self-delusion, by which, as we have
seen, she sanctifies her villainy, is certainly one of these variations, as is her apparently successful employment of the
story of Maggie's downfall to excuse her drunkenness—on
forty-two occasions—to the police. The greatest element in
her survival, however, is not so much a matter of diversity as
it is the functioning of an enormously powerful will to survive, perhaps best illustrated by the scene in which, fiercely
drunk and barely able to keep her feet, she is surrounded by
a group of taunting youths—much as a wounded elk might
be encircled by a wolf pack—and summons almost magically
the strength to reach her lair unscathed.

JIMMIE

The most eloquent display of diversity in *Maggie* belongs to
Jimmie. Soundly reared in a climate of familial antagonism,
he enters manhood with a clear understanding of the nature
of reality. "He studied human nature in the gutter, and found
it no worse than he thought he had reason to believe it. He
never conceived a respect for the world, because he had
begun with no idols that it had smashed." Strength and fear-
lessness he discovered to be the equipment of survival;
weakness, he found, was displayed not merely by those beneath him, but also by those apparently above him: "To him
fine raiment was allied to weakness, and all good coats covered faint hearts. He and his order were kings, to a certain
extent, over the men of untarnished clothes, because these
latter dreaded perhaps to be either killed or laughed at." He
explicitly recognizes the significance of the struggle for existence and his own role in it. The "creatures" of the world
"were all trying to take advantage of him," and it thus became necessary "to quarrel on all possible occasions." As a
truck driver he came to look with contempt upon passenger-
carrying streetcars. These he characterizes as "bugs," while
pedestrians are "pestering flies." They are his prey, and he is

the "common prey of all energetic officials." The one thing in the world that he admires is a fire engine drawn by "leaping horses" and capable of overturning a streetcar: a mighty symbol of animal power, the fittest, perhaps, of the beasts. Like his mother he is always able to adopt such variations as may become necessary to justify his behavior. For a time he finds it difficult to reconcile his denunciation of Maggie and his attack on Pete, her seducer, with his own rejection of the woman he has himself seduced. But the moral dilemma is of brief duration, and the difficulty largely vanishes as he discovers that fighting with Pete on behalf of Maggie is wasteful since unrelated to his own struggle—to the demands of which nothing must be sacrificed: just before the fight, Jimmie's anonymous comrade in arms remonstrates: "Gee! What's d' use?" When the fight is broken up and a policeman collars his comrade, Jimmie, starting to go to the rescue, changes his mind. "Ah," he says, "what's d' use?" The lesson is well learned. Subsequently, upon being visited by the fleeting notion that Maggie "would have been more firmly good had she better known how," he immediately recognizes the compromise involved in maintaining such a viewpoint. "He threw it hastily aside." The irony here is of course that "learning the lesson" consists simply in reverting to a more primitive level of behavior.

In our first meetings with Pete it appears that he is in all respects a perfect example of one destined to survive. But actually, as we soon discover, he is possessed of a fatal ambivalence of attitude. Although he has been to some extent Jimmie's teacher in the ways of the jungle and has the physical prowess to enable him, even more than Jimmie, to withstand the hazards of the struggle, his devotion to the cause of his survival has led him into an aberration—an "unprofitable variation": concern for the regard of others and for an external standard by which to measure his behavior. Unlike Jimmie and Jimmie's mother, Pete cannot adopt the variations necessary to provide his own justifications for his actions, and thereby achieve self-sufficiency. When he fails to win a goodnight kiss from Maggie on their first date he reflects to himself with far greater concern than is healthy: "Gee . . . I wonner if I've been played fer a duffer." And later, after Maggie's death, stricken by an emotion suspiciously resembling guilt, he feels obliged to entertain a party of prostitutes from whom he drunkenly requests frequent assur-

ances that "I'm goo' f'ler." That such behavior is entirely inimical to survival is fully demonstrated by his guests of the
evening, who lose no time making for the exit when he finally drinks himself to the floor. "The women screamed in
disgust and drew back their skirts. 'Come akin,' cried one,
starting up angrily, 'let's get out of here.'" Once again the
irony is quite apparent. It becomes doubly so here, since it
generally requires a rodent or an insect to affect ladies in
this manner, and on this occasion the ladies in question are
not really ladies at all.

MAGGIE: A TRIUMPH

Several remarks are to be made [about *Maggie*] and first
in regard to its *art*, which is an effect of intense pressure
and nearly perfect detachment. No American work of its
length had driven the reader so hard; in none had the author
remained so persistently invisible behind his creation. The
incongruity of these qualities forces our attention to the
strangeness—the daring and ambition—of Crane's attempt.
. . . The banal story . . . had to be given heroic and pathetic
stature and yet not falsified. At the same time, its melodramatic character called for disguise under an air of flatness
and casualness. Furthermore Crane had to rely on loose,
episodic structure—except once or twice he would never use
any other. And no passion such as revenge or love or greed
could dominate the fable. If in these unpropitious circumstances he achieved in *Maggie* a sense of inevitability, one
may well wonder how he did it. The word Howells was to use
for this triumph of Crane was a good one, namely, "Greek."

John Berryman, *Stephen Crane,* 1950.

It should be emphasized that regardless of the degree to
which each succeeds in the struggle for existence, all of the
characters thus far discussed, with the exception of the
baby, recognize with great constancy both the absolute
value of survival and the certainty that the struggle is the
sole path to its maintenance. In the specific tale of Maggie's
downfall Crane comments on this certainty by presenting
the case of one who attempts to remain aloof from the
struggle. It is not that Maggie totally fails to recognize the
nature of the world, but that her vision is a dual one. When
first encountered she is engaged in what might be termed
the brutal performance of an act of compassion: we see her

leading the baby, Tommie, small and bedraggled, through the press of a crowded street, now jerking on his arm so that he falls, now jerking him upright. The act of compassion—the leading of the child—belongs to a world which is related to the novel only through its appearance in Maggie's dreams and in the procession of make-believe images that she comes to witness in her brief life. It is a world in which there is love and in which people depend upon and assume responsibility for one another—a world much like the one that Darwin projected for highly civilized, "social" man. The brutality that characterizes the act of compassion belongs to the actual world in which Maggie must live, in which survival is the sole absolute value, and the struggle the one path to survival.

MAGGIE'S VISION

In what may be called the four stages of her journey through the novel, the poles of her dual vision compete irregularly for Maggie's belief. In the first stage, that of childhood, she is a realist, fashioning her image of the world from the object lessons to which she is daily exposed. The actual world is brought very close. The other world is a vague possibility on the fringe of consciousness, reinforced during these early years by the single incident—and it receives ironic treatment—of her acquiring a flower for Tommie's burial. Her tentative profferings of affection and compassion are rejected by Jimmie, and she of course receives no affection or compassion, either from him or from her miserable, drunken mother and father. It is therefore only to be expected that in her growing up she should become inured to "a world of hardships and insults." The object lessons have done their job.

But as she begins the second stage of her journey, now grown to womanhood, there persists together with her awareness of the actual world a sense of the possibility of escape to the other world. Thus her fashioning of a lambrequin, a pathetic symbol of beauty, an attempt at adorning her life and changing her world. Thus, too, her envy of "elegance and soft palm," her craving for "adornments of persons," and her aspiration to the "culture and refinement" she sees on the stage.

In her idealization of Pete, Maggie attempts to unite the poles of her dual image: "Here was a formidable man who disdained the strength of the world full of fists. Here was one who had contempt for brass-clothed power; one whose knuckles could ring defiantly against the granite of law." Pete is admired because he represents a promise both of the possibility of escape and of the power to deal with the world of hardships and insults on its own terms. He leads Maggie to a galaxy of make-believe images: to cabarets, museums, a freak-show, and particularly to theaters, where "the poor and virtuous eventually overcame the wealthy and wicked"—while a choir sang "Joy to the World." But Pete is equally Maggie's champion in the actual world. There were "people who were afraid of him," and he is capable of translating into action her silent wish to "see somebody entangle their fingers in the oily beard of the fat foreigner"—the owner of the sweatshop in which she works.

In the third stage of her journey Maggie suddenly loses all contact with the actual world. Unable to bear any longer the misery of her life at home, particularly the ill use she suffers at the hands of her mother, she gives herself physically to Pete, and from the moment she is accepted by him her sense of the possibility of escape to the other world dominates her awareness of the world in which she is condemned to live. She speaks to Pete of love, comes to depend on him, puts her life into his charge. "She imagined a future rose-tinted because of its distance from all that she had experienced before." She actually adopts refinements ("unprofitable variations"), shrinking from physical contact with the painted women whose ranks she will soon enter (again, irony at work).

When Pete leaves her, which he does as casually as a sated stallion, Maggie is not, as might be expected, jolted back to her vision of the actual world. She is now too thoroughly committed to her yearning for the other to do anything but increase desperately her efforts to reach it. Thus she goes home on a fool's errand to seek forgiveness from her mother and Jimmie. When they scornfully send her on her way she seeks out Pete and attempts to make him accept responsibility for the charge she has put in his hands. When he tells her to "go to hell!" she goes instead in search of the "grace of God," and it is only when she has been rebuffed by the anonymous gentleman of "the chaste black coat"—whom she has chosen to symbolize that grace—that she appears to end her search.

ESCAPE

In the fourth stage of her journey Maggie at first appears to have returned with a vengeance to her vision of the actual world. At last, it would seem, she has come to accept the certainty that its laws are inexorable, and in conducting her life in accordance with those laws (it is of particular interest that she has chosen to make capital of animal necessity) she appears to have been eminently successful. We observe that she is well-dressed and expert at least in the preliminary techniques of her newly adopted profession, and we can only conclude that she has made a success of it. But then we suddenly find that all is not as it appears, that what actually confronts us in this remarkable reversal of vision and behavior is another instance of irony. For Maggie, as we now see, has retained a fatal measure of her vision of the other world, and it now appears to her unreasoning consciousness that escape to it can be accomplished only by means of a forcible exit from the actual one. Consequently, on a rainy night, with business slack, she jumps in the river and drowns.

In another novel Maggie's action might have been a symbolic triumph for her vision of the other world, and palpable evidence of the possibility of escape from control by the laws governing the actual one. Indeed, it might perhaps seem that she has beaten the system, for there are very few animals in the uncivilized state of sufficient will to take their own lives. But the final irony is that Maggie's illusion—unlike those of her mother and brother—is unprofitable; it substitutes for the absolute value of survival. The most incredible self-deception, as we have seen, is perfectly all right—that is, useful—as long as it comprises a profitable variation and thereby aids in a successful prosecution of the struggle. In Maggie's case, however, since it serves to remove her from the struggle, illusion is an unprofitable variation; and we are left to conclude not only that Crane envisions no haven on the other side of Maggie's watery grave, but also that by her action she has contravened the "morality" of life.

Maggie's story is, of course, a very sad one, and it is perhaps shocking to think that Crane is out of sympathy with her ill-fortune. But clearly he is; or rather the matter of sympathy is irrelevant to his scheme for the novel. He has attained sufficient objectivity to be rid of the necessity—indeed of the opportunity—for judgment, and *Maggie*, examined on its own terms, offers no suggestion of alternatives to the struggle for existence as the single appropriate metaphor for the life of human beings. In the world order of this novel, either one's life conforms to the demands of the struggle, or it is extinguished. There are no exceptions, and we have no cause to suspect that there could be any. Thus can the Naturalism of *Maggie* be identified as a rigorous, Darwinistic determinism, and a denial, if not of the existence of a world beyond, of man's ability to contact it.

Stylistic Weakness in *Maggie*

Arno Karlen

Critic Arno Karlen takes Stephen Crane's first short novel to task. Quoting passages throughout *Maggie*, Karlen identifies Crane's lack of control and reliance on melodrama to conclude that *Maggie* is a deeply flawed work.

In his earliest fiction, Crane already showed his gifts and weaknesses clearly. He had a brilliant, unorthodox ear for far-flung analogies. Friends recorded that he spoke of an old egg having a "snarling smell," and that he called Mark Twain's *A Connecticut Yankee* "as inappropriate as a drunken bride." In the opening pages of his short first novel, *Maggie*, he produced such unpredictable beauties as:

> Over on the island a worm of yellow convicts came from the shadow of a gray ominous building and crawled slowly along the river's bank.

> The little boy ran to the halls, shrieking like a monk in an earthquake.

> He became a young man of leather. He lived some red years without laboring.

Within the same pages, Crane produced such strained and inaccurate sentences as:

> Blows dealt in the fight were enlarged to catapultian power.

> The broken furniture, the grimy walls ... appeared before her and began to take on a potential aspect.

> In front of the gruesome doorway he met a lurching figure.

Crane could not resist modifiers. Some were brilliant, some appalling—poor verbal shortcuts and hasty guesses—but almost always there were too many:

> He glanced over into the vacant lot in which the little raving boys from Devil's Row seethed about the shrieking and tearful child from Rum Alley.

Excerpted from Arno Karlen, "The Craft of Stephen Crane," which originally appeared in the *Georgia Review*, vol. 27 (Fall 1987); ©1974 by The University of Georgia. Reprinted by permission of the author and the *Georgia Review*.

As the sullen-eyed man, followed by the blood-covered boy, drew near, the little girl burst into reproachful cries.

Maggie also shows a weakness for words that tell instead of show—dead wood of the "nice" and "bad" variety. When Crane didn't have something inspired, he used whatever was handy, especially superlatives. The words "lurid," "gruesome," "formidable," "tremendous," "furious," crowd the tumid sentences. Desperate to convince, Crane produced an atmosphere of grotesquerie in which everything was bigger than life, like a violent shadow play. No one speaks in the opening pages of *Maggie;* everyone shouts, bellows, roars. Yet amid all this . . . lie sentences that are little masterpieces of the most subtle and difficult prose effects—rhythm, assonance, alliteration—and full of premeditated irony or menacing beauty.

He paced placidly along with the applewood emblem of serenity clenched between his teeth.

Above all things he despised obvious Christians and ciphers with the chrysanthemums of aristocracy in their buttonholes.

The building quivered and creaked from the weight of humanity stamping about in its bowels.

Such beautiful rhythms, though, are often succeeded by clanking monotony, especially when several sentences in a row have the same structure, length, and cadence:

The urchin raised his voice in defiance to his parent, and continued his attacks. The babe bawled tremendously, protesting with great violence. During his sister's hasty maneuver, he was dragged by the arm.

Crane often strung together passive verbs and past tenses that leave the verb "to be" droning in one's ear:

He was throwing stones at howling urchins from Devil's Row, who were circling madly about the heap and pelting him. His infantile countenance was livid with the fury of battle. His small body was writhing in the delivery of oaths.

Sometimes the references and time sequence are confusingly tangled:

Once, when a lady had dropped her purse on the sidewalk, the gnarled woman had grabbed it and smuggled it with great dexterity beneath her cloak. When she was arrested she had cursed the lady into a partial swoon, and with her aged limbs, twisted from rheumatism, had kicked the breath out of a huge policeman whose conduct upon that occasion she referred to when she said, "The police, damn 'em!"

And then all the glories and all the fumbling combine in one long sentence:

> Above the muffled roar of conversation, the dismal wailing of babies at night, the thumping of feet in unseen corridors and rooms, and the sound of varied hoarse shoutings in the street and the rattling of wheels over cobbles, they heard the screams of the child and the roars of the mother die away to a feeble moaning and a subdued bass muttering.

WOODEN CLUMSINESS

Crane's writing always suffered from occasional lapses into wooden clumsiness or rigidity, and often the cause was pompous diction. The Naturalists inherited more from their Romantic forebears than they could admit. The intrigue with local color, dialect, and street language was an extension of Romantic exoticism; the taste for the strange, the brutal, the frankly sexual, moved from Gipsy camps and South Sea islands to the industrial slums. The Goncourt brothers, students of Oriental art and eighteenth-century courtesans, went walking the poor quarters of Paris to collect details of squalor, vulgarity, and violence, then went home to polish their notes with *frissons* not only of compassion but of fascinated disgust. The works of many great Naturalists, including Crane's, abound with sentimentality and vague, passionate effusions. Their very unconcern about techniques was Romantic, an assumption that powerful feelings and deep truths could be conveyed by the brute force of their being, almost despite craft. After all, it was a Romantic who said, long before Zola or Howells, that truth is beauty, beauty truth.

When one word mars in mid-course the suppleness and glitter of one of Crane's sentences, the reason is often that the word is self-consciously literary. Changing the highfalutin word to idiomatic speech rescues the sentence, as in these parenthetical substitutions in sentences from *Maggie:*

> As he neared the spot where the little boys strove (fought), he regarded them listlessly.

> His infantile countenance (childish face) was livid with the fury of battle.

> The old woman was a gnarled and leathery personage (was gnarled and leathery). . . .

Perhaps another reason for this inflated diction was Crane's desire to keep a good Naturalist's scientific distance from his subject. The result of such a tone tends to be the sort of stuff social scientists indulge in so often—saying "overt expressions of interpersonal attitudes in societal interaction" when they mean "the way people act." But Crane sometimes used diffidence and high diction to achieve some of his finest effects. His pose of neutrality and his polysyllables could be tools of irony, mocking the trivial by forcing it into full-dress costume. Again, from *Maggie:*

> He sat on the table of the Johnson home, and dangled his checked legs with an enticing nonchalance. His hair was curled down over his forehead in an oiled bang. His pugged nose seemed to revolt from contact with a bristling moustache of short, wire-like hairs. His blue double-breasted coat, edged with black braid, was buttoned close to a red puff tie, and his patent leather shoes looked like weapons.

> His mannerisms stamped him as a man who had a correct sense of his personal superiority. There were valor and contempt for circumstances in the glance of his eye. He waved his hands like a man of the world who dismisses religion and philosophy, and says "Rats." He had certainly seen everything, and with each curl of his lip he declared that it amounted to nothing. Maggie thought he must be a very "elegant" bartender.

One character after another becomes pathetically comical when Crane presents him with dispassionate, formal voice. The word "reverent" may have never held as much vitriol and pathos as in the last sentence of the chapter devoted to

A DEPRESSING NOVEL

We should classify Mr. Crane as a rather promising writer of the animalistic school. His types are mainly human beings of the order which makes us regret the power of literature to portray them. Not merely are they low, but there is little that is interesting in them. We resent the sense that we must at certain points resemble them. Even the old mother is not made pathetic in a human way; her son disgusts us so that we have small power of sympathy with her left. Maggie it is impossible to weep over. We can feel only that it is a pity that the gutter is so dirty, and turn in another direction. In short, Mr. Crane's art is to us very depressing. Of course, there is always the crushing reply that one who does not love art for the sake of art is a poor devil, not worth writing for. But we do not; we do not even love literature for its own sake.

The Nation, July 2, 1896.

Maggie's brother Jimmie, the truck driver who "menaced mankind at the intersections of streets."

> Nevertheless, he had, on a certain star-lit evening, said wonderingly and quite reverently, "Deh moon looks like hell, don't it?"

Finally, *Maggie* leaves a memory of brilliant effects and glaring failures jumbled together, of heavy-handed irony, telegraphed punches, exquisite humor, melodrama, and verbal audacity. Crane begins fortissimo and then keeps straining for a crescendo, confusing volume with the power of harmony. But you can act no louder than your loudest. Typically, when Crane had a chance to revise *Maggie* for a second edition, he hesitated on the grounds that improving it on a second try was "dishonest." As usual he confused sincerity and craft.

Crane's Use of Biblical Parables in *Maggie*

William Bysshe Stein

Critic William Bysshe Stein has published several articles on Stephen Crane in various academic journals. In this selection, Stein focuses on Crane's use of New Testament parables in *Maggie*. Stein argues that Crane inverts many of the parables of Jesus; his message becomes not salvation but the hopelessness of Maggie's situation.

The rigid naturalistic interpretations of *Maggie,* so popular in some critical circles today, obscure the universal implications of Crane's dramatic re-creation of Bowery existence. It is not enough, for instance, to say that the novel is the sum of "innocence thwarted and betrayed by environment."[1] Such a categorical statement implies that Crane's view of reality is unalterably objective, concerned only with the transcription of calculable sociological data. Actually his creative imagination is deeply stirred by religious aspects of the setting. This is seen in a recurrent pattern of symbolic moral situations which is inspired by the New Testament.

Here, of course, Crane's background is the point at issue. Reared in a confining religious atmosphere (his father was a Methodist minister and his mother a newspaper reporter of church activities), he unconsciously was trained to think in the ideological framework of Christianity. Even in rebellion against its expression in institutional religion, he could not completely subdue its incontrovertible ethical affirmations. We can see, for example, his patent detestation of mission evangelism in *Maggie,* and we can understand his impatience with its blatant self-righteousness. But, on the other hand, he introduces certain scenes and incidents which,

1. *Stephen Crane: Stories and Tales*, ed. Robert W. Stallman (Vintage Books; New York, 1955), p. 7, introduction to the Bowery Tales

Excerpted from William Bysshe Stein, "New Testament Inversions in Crane's *Maggie,*" *Modern Language Notes*, vol. 73 (April 1958), pp. 268–72; ©1958 The Johns Hopkins University Press. Reprinted with permission of the publisher.

though they do not beg attention, are nevertheless manifestations of an intuitive loyalty to the redemptive love of the Gospels. In the opening chapter of the book there is, I think, evidence of this. His juxtaposition of the violent scuffle in the alley with the tableau of human callousness illustrates what I mean: "From a window of an apartment-house that uprose from amid squat stables there leaned a curious woman. Some labourers, unloading a scow at a dock at the river, paused for a moment and regarded the fight. The engineer of a passive tugboat hung lazily over a railing and watched. Over on the island a worm of yellow convicts came from the shadow of a building and crawled slowly along the river's bank." These phlegmatic onlookers, so carefully foreshortened against the background of a prison, epitomize the indifference of a society familiar with violence and crime. But at the same time their moral unconcern represents the degradation of the values of love and compassion in their daily lives. This is to say that Crane's visualization of the heartlessness of human relationships in this scene takes note of the paralysis of Christianity in this environment and in the world.

MAGGIE'S ENTITLEMENT TO FORGIVENESS

In effect, his scenic logic argues that human nature is depraved; but he counterpoints this attitude with an argument to the contrary which promises a deliverance from this amoral state. The complete title of the novel, *Maggie: A Girl of the Streets,* constitutes an initiation into the function of this device of irony. The name Maggie is deliberately equated with the practice of prostitution, but it is also, in context at least, suggestively proposed as a diminutive of Magdalene. This etymology, of course, is not correct, but here the association is almost instinctive for anyone acquainted with the parables. Since Crane presupposes, as all of us must, that in our culture man has been taught to make sense out of his experience in terms of the Christian myth, then the title should excite our sympathy instead of indignation. The heroine, in other words, is entitled to forgiveness like her counterpart in the New Testament. Crane has in mind, I think, Maggie's quite pardonable sin of assuming that love will redeem all, and at this juncture she metamorphoses into Magdalene: "Wherefore I say unto Thee, Her sins which are many, are forgiven; for she loved much: but

to whom little is forgiven, the *same* loveth little."[2] This interpretation may seem to run counter to the opinions about
Christ expressed by Crane in his poetry; yet his quick sympathy with prostitutes is an impulse of his moral condition-
ing—a much sounder gauge of his spiritual values, it seems
to me, than the sophomoric heresies which dialectically
shape some of his poems. Then, too, the novel was written
before he began to connect his aggressive moral impatience
with the scientific naturalism which enveloped the literary
world of his day.

In any event, without too much difficulty this interpretive
approach to the title can be applied to certain crucial
episodes in the narrative. Jimmy's attempt to convince his
mother that Maggie ought to be permitted to return home
after her seduction results in a depressing burlesque of the
Prodigal Son. By treating the incident humorously, Crane
horrifyingly enhances the sadism of the mother. Unable to
explain rationally his instinctive desire to protect his sister,
Jimmy can only justify it by disclaiming its connection with
Christian morality: "'Well, I didn't mean none of dis prod'gal
bus'ness anyway.'" She, however, triumphantly refutes the
validity of this precedent with the crushing rejoinder: "'It
wa'n't no prod'gal daughter, yeh fool.'" And reducing Jimmy
to impotent silence, she proceeds to revel in the opportunity
for abuse which Maggie's inevitable return promises: "The
mother's eyes gloated on the scene which her imagination
called before her." This inversion and its implications are
obvious, but they lend sanction to my belief that the un-
voiced inspiration of the novel is Crane's distressed insight
into the abandonment of Christian love by his culture.

THE GOOD SAMARITAN

This perception is forcefully embodied in another important
segment of the action. It involves Maggie's quest for salvation after her rejection by Peter, and is an adaptation of another New Testament motif. The minister's lack of mercy in
this case parallels the response of the priest in the parable of
the Good Samaritan. Maggie, seeking the "grace of God," decides to accost "a stout gentleman in a silk hat and chaste
black coat," but he makes "a convulsive movement and
save[s] his respectability by a vigorous side-step." A glance

2. Luke 7: 47

MELODRAMA AS TECHNIQUE

Critic Thomas A. Gullason argues that the melodramatic passages in Crane's Maggie *that are often criticized are in fact intentional and positive.*

Both tragedy and melodrama, with melodrama predominating, exist in Stephen Crane's *Maggie* (1893). On the surface, they suggest that Crane was working at cross-purposes. There is a limited sense of Aristotelian tragedy in the novel: in the representation of and the appeal to the emotions of pity and fear; in the compact, dramatic, and scenic structure. Tragic heroes and heroines, however—that is, people who are noble and "better"—are nowhere to be found. Moreover, there is no real movement from happiness to misery (Maggie's happiness is short-lived), only movement from misery to more misery. There is nothing to make one "marvel." Instead there is much that recalls melodrama: sensation, violence, terror, and shock, seemingly for their own sake; mawkish sentiment; vulgar rhetoric; stereotyped and one-dimensional people and situations; exaggerated actions and reactions that waver between the grotesque and the ludicrous.

Periodic references have been made to tragedy and melodrama in the criticism of Stephen Crane's first novel, yet little evidence has been presented to explain their positive values and strengths. No one has advanced the idea, for example, that Crane—a very precocious writer—was purposely mixing the two genres in the one work in order to reflect a tragicomic world. This perspective on the novel exposes finer and more subtle shades of Crane's talent; and while it does not transform *Maggie* into a great novel, it makes it more substantial.

Thomas A. Gullason, *Maggie: A Girl of the Streets*. Norton Critical Edition, 1979.

at the circumstances of the parable will suffice to establish their relationship with this episode: "A certain man . . . fell among thieves, which stripped him of his raiment, and wounded *him*, and departed, leaving him half dead. And by chance there came a certain priest that way; and when he saw him, he passed by on the other side."[3] Ordinarily one would, I think, tend to limit this parody to Crane's contempt for the clergy and their fastidiously cultivated piety. But the satirical probe strikes deeper. It penetrates to the real cause of the degeneration of love in human affairs—the betrayal of Christ by his ministry.

3. Luke 10: 30–31

Still another episode evolves out of the religious matrix of the artist's inspiration, the last scene in the novel. Mary's affected sorrow over Maggie's death is made painfully obvious, but once again Crane assumes that the reader will associate the travesty of bereavement with its archetypal counterpart. I refer, of course, to the conventional representation of the Virgin lamenting over the body of Christ after the crucifixion. Crane's re-creation of the depraved Pietà of the slums is contrived to comment ironically upon the mother's name, but it also functions to cast the black pall of an irredeemable Good Friday upon the culture which he criticizes. For, contrary to the critics who argue that *Maggie* is a victim of her environment, he dramatizes the key scenes of her pathetic fate against the background of man's defection from the redemptive love of Christianity as it is crystallized in John's record of the Savior's conversation after his betrayal by Judas: "A new commandment I give unto you, That ye love one another; as I have loved you, that ye also love one another."[4] Maggie, in short, is crucified by the same forces of hate in human nature that destroyed Christ. Fittingly the concluding chapter of the novel is characterized by the repetition of the word black in contrast with the violent colors of life in the earlier chapters. In this way Crane emphasizes the advent of the Black Friday which can become Good Friday only when it ensures salvation. But, in his perspective, this miraculous transformation cannot occur. The darkness of hate is fixed for ever in time.

OTHER NEW TESTAMENT REFERENCES

And considering the symbolic function of the names of Maggie and Mary, it may not be farfetched to ascribe a similar meaning to the names of Peter and Jimmy. Simon Peter and James were the two disciples who accompanied Christ on the road to Calvary. Even the young Tommy who dies in his infancy may be a vague reflection of his doubting namesake in the New Testament. His death, in any event, seems to prove that Thomas intuitively foresaw the failure of the law of love as in later history it is interpreted by the new Marys, and Peters, and Jameses. Confirmation of Crane's preoccupation with the nature of human and divine love is sardonically recorded in the name he chooses for the unscrupulous

4. John 13: 34

prostitute, Nell. The new Helen of Troy mocks the meaning of love in her scarlet arrogance, reversing the downfall not only of her Green congener but of the Whore of Babylon in The Revelation, the prototypal scarlet woman. She sheds no tears, she wastes no pity, she shows no remorse. She lives in the spirit of the new law of venal love which Crane proclaims to rule the world.

This conviction, enhanced by immersion in the destructive element of personal experience, perhaps explains why in his later fiction religious images, for the most part, serve as simple correlatives of irony. Crane seems to lose even his provisional faith in the symbolic machinery of Christian salvation. When Maggie's innocent dream of love died, something may be said to have died in his soul.

Recognizing the Two Voices in Crane's Poetry

Max Westbrook

Although Stephen Crane's reputation rests on his novels and short stories, he also wrote unusual and unique poetry reminiscent of Emily Dickinson. His poems are short, symbolic, and typically pessimistic about humanity's relationship to God. In the following article, critic Max Westbrook analyzes Crane's poetry further, claiming that Crane uses two voices; the voice of perspective, which he affirms, and the voice of arrogance, which he mocks. Hearing these two voices allows the reader to discern Crane's meaning.

Amy Lowell, writing on Stephen Crane's poetry, concludes that he usually "sees only purposeless effort" in the universe. She believes that the affirmative poems he did write are atypical. They are the product of a temporary mood which Crane, a "boy, spiritually killed by neglect," could not sustain in an alien world. Daniel G. Hoffman, who knows Crane died of tuberculosis and not of neglect, believes that the poems are committed to an "heroic ideal" derived in part from Emerson. Hoffman's conclusion, however, is that Crane

> makes us feel the reality of a universe where force is law, where love is doom, where God is cold, where man's lot is fated misery, where hope is narrowed to the possibility of courage, and the reward of courage is self-sacrifice.

The conclusions of Lowell and Hoffman represent the critical consensus: Crane could not maintain his affirmative beliefs in a universe he found to be, in the final analysis, deterministic. It is granted that his experiments are a significant contribution to the development of modern poetry, but his accomplishment is said to be undermined by his inability to sustain a coherent world view.

All poets, of course, have temporary moods, employ different and even conflicting themes. The critics, however, have

Excerpted from Max Westbrook, "Stephen Crane's Poetry: Perspective and Arrogance," *Bucknell Review*, vol. 11 (December 1963), pp. 24–34. Reprinted by permission of Bucknell University Press/Associated University Presses.

not questioned Crane's right to use conflicting, themes; they have questioned his coherence. It is my contention that Crane's poetry does cohere, but in a way no one has yet noticed. The practice has been to assume that the poems have a single protagonist—everyman, or perhaps Crane himself—whose experiences represent man's relation to ultimate reality. The hopes and beliefs of this protagonist are sometimes affirmed, sometimes mocked. Values are sometimes real, sometimes illusory. And thus the natural conclusion has been that Crane's world view is arbitrary, unrealized. Crane's readers, however, have failed to distinguish two quite different voices in the poems. The voice of perspective, with reasonable consistency, is affirmed; the voice of arrogance, without exception, is mocked. Behind both voices lies a single and coherent standard of values.

The differentiation of two voices need not be proscriptive. Crane's vision is not that pat. Nonetheless, it can be shown that Crane uses the voice of perspective and the voice of arrogance to make value judgments that are of structural importance to his poetry. The voice of perspective draws Crane's deepest sympathy; it is characterized by humility, kindness, a quiet determination, and by a consistent belief in a truth which is symbolic, elusive, but always real. The voice of arrogance—representing the values Crane attacked in his prose and fiction as well as in his poetry—is characterized by pride, dogmatism, often by an aggressive manner, and by a stubborn insistence on a literal truth. A study of these voices, the most recurrent ones in Crane's poetry, shows that beneath hope and despair there lies an essential unity.

A PESSIMISTIC VIEW

Crane's emphasis on pessimistic themes cannot be denied. The anthologies have rightly made famous *War Is Kind* XXI, in which the universe is indifferent to man; and *Black Riders* VI, in which "the ship of the world" is allowed to wander "for ever rudderless." Also well known are poems on the suffering of common men, the hypocrisy of men of esteem, and the innate wickedness of all men. If these poems constitute a balanced and judicious selection, Lowell and Hoffman are right. Deterministic and naturalistic themes offer no rationale for affirmation. Such poems, however, describe only part of the universe as Crane saw it.

That universe includes *War Is Kind* II, which praises the

humanistic values of patience, gentleness, and brotherhood. It includes *War Is Kind* XXV, in which God is expressed by symbolic "Songs of carmine, violet, green, gold." *Black Riders* XL and XLII attack what so many of Crane's critics would have us believe he held sacrosanct: the idea that man's failures should be blamed on environment. There is even a surprising affinity between Crane the realist and Emerson the transcendentalist, an affinity which lies in the religious legacy Crane took over—unconsciously perhaps—from his devout family. Crane often attacks naivete, sentimentality, and hypocrisy; and it is true that the indifference of nature and the destructive power of environment are favorite themes; but the basic values of his personal creed are love, kindness, and sympathy for human suffering.

Crane's handling of humanistic values is Emersonian, specifically, in that the real cannot be institutionalized. The real, as in *Black Riders* XXVIII, is better approached with sensitiveness and humility than with aggressive confidence:

"Truth," said a traveller,
"Is a rock, a mighty fortress;
Often have I been to it,
Even to its highest tower,
From whence the world looks black."

"Truth," said a traveller,
"Is a breath, a wind,
A shadow, a phantom;
Long have I pursued it,
But never have I touched
The hem of its garment."

And I believed the second traveller;
For truth was to me
A breath, a wind,
A shadow, a phantom,
And never had I touched
The hem of its garment.

The poem offers a convenient means of demonstrating my thesis, for in it we hear both the voice of perspective and the voice of arrogance. The first traveller believes that truth is, metaphorically, a "rock," a "fortress," something man can discover in a fixed shape and identify with certainty. If the first traveller is speaking for Crane, then the charge of incoherence is valid, for the negativism of the first traveller's discovery is clearly incompatible with Crane's affirmative poems. The first traveller, however, is wrong. The truth is, in the metaphor of the second traveller, a "shadow," a "phantom," something man can never discover in a fixed shape, something man can never encompass or exhaust. The truth exists, as suggested by the refrain "The hem of its garment," but it exists as an elusive "shadow," not as a fixed "rock" or institutionalized "fortress." The humble and resolute faith of the second traveller marks him as one who has gained perspective through his awareness of the nature of reality. The first traveller, by contrast, concludes that "the world looks black," a negativism which reveals, not the reality of determinism in Crane's poetic world, but the error of the first traveller's own concept of the real.

Believing that the truth is more accurately described as a "shadow" than as a "rock," Crane places a high value on the virtue of humility. Man cannot be arrogant about the grasp he has on a "shadow." In protesting against false gods and cruel men, the man of perspective may become bitter, but he is always humble before the truth, and for this reason he is never mocked. If he is defeated, his downfall is recorded with sympathy, his efforts have not been without purpose. Crane's irony is used to attack the man whose attitude toward the truth is characterized by aggressiveness, dogmatism, conceit—the man whose efforts, therefore, are futile.

In support of her more customary reading of Crane's poetry, Amy Lowell cites *Black Riders* XXIV:

I saw a man pursuing the horizon;
Round and round they sped.
I was disturbed at this;
I accosted the man.
"It is futile," I said,
"You can never—"
"You lie," he cried,
And ran on.

If the distinction between the voice of perspective and the voice of arrogance is valid, then it is a mistake to read this poem as an example of determinism or purposelessness. Crane is not a determinist in "I Saw a Man" and an Emersonian in "'Truth,' Said a Traveller"; nor is there a shift in world view from one poem to the other. The furious pursuit "round and round" describes one man's gross misconception of the nature of truth and the consequent purposelessness of *his* efforts, not the purposelessness of all human striving after higher values.

The quiet observer in "I Saw a Man" tries to speak, only to

be interrupted. The man "pursuing the horizon" will not listen. The quiet observer wants to explain what his counterpart does explain in "'Truth,' Said a Traveller": you cannot chase the truth down mad-dog fashion; you cannot even touch "The hem of its garment." Man must be humble and resolute before a truth that is elusive and symbolic.

RECOGNIZING TWO VOICES

Recognition of the two major voices in Crane's poetry offers a number of advantages. It suggests a new and I think more convincing interpretation for many poems, especially for poems in which the speaker has not yet achieved perspective but is beginning to learn:

> A man saw a ball of gold in the sky;
> He climbed for it,
> And eventually he achieved it—
> It was clay.
>
> Now this is the strange part:
> When the man went to the earth
> And looked again,
> Lo, there was the ball of gold.
> Now this is the strange part:
> It was a ball of gold.
> Ay, by the heavens, it was a ball of gold.

The poem (*Black Riders* XXXV) has been said to mean that man's belief in ultimate values is a mockery, an interpretation which requires that the last line be taken ironically. The tone of the poem, however, is objective, calm. It is characterized by that perspective Crane associates with an awareness of the elusive nature of truth. Thus a more satisfactory paraphrase is suggested: the value represented by the ball of gold exists, but it must be seen in perspective—obliquely, from a distance—or else be distorted. It cannot be climbed for in the sky any more than it can be chased to the horizon; man cannot get his hands on a truth which is symbolic.

Recognition of the two voices, furthermore, enables one to include in his reading of Crane certain poems which have been slighted by the anthologies or dismissed by the critics as the product of a temporary mood. Crane's so-called affirmative and negativistic poems can be seen to describe different voices heard in the same universe. *Black Riders* XXXIX is typical of this group:

> The livid lightnings flashed in the clouds;
> The leaden thunders crashed.

A worshipper raised his arm.
"Hearken! hearken! The voice of God!"

"Not so," said a man.
"The voice of God whispers in the heart
So softly
That the soul pauses,
Making no noise,
And strives for these melodies,
Distant, sighing, like faintest breath,
And all the being is still to hear."

If the reader distinguishes the voice of perspective from the voice of arrogance, he sees that the worshipper is made absurd by a flaw in his own concept of the real, not by a flaw in the real itself. Listening for God in thunder is just as futile as chasing truth to the horizon. As shown by "The livid lightnings," the mistaken and therefore futile beliefs of man can exist in the same poem—in the same world—with a meaningful belief in higher values.

Failure to distinguish the two voices has led critics to impose a preconceived theology on Crane's poems, to assume that if God is indifferent then man's pursuit of truth must be without purpose, and the God who "whispers in the heart" must be a comfort merely, not a reality. In Crane's poetic world, however, there are two Gods. One, the Old Testament God, is portrayed unsympathetically as a God of pride who judges man coldly, even cruelly. Crane associates Him frequently with the conventional church, sometimes with a corrupt morality that ignores human suffering, sometimes with the theme of nature's indifference. The second God is an internal conscience, a God who speaks only to the individual. Both Gods are forcefully described in *Black Riders* LIII. The Old Testament God, a "puffing braggart" who stamps "across the sky" with "loud swagger," is threatened with curses. The inner God, by contrast, is treated with reverence: "Ah, sooner would I die / Than see tears in those eyes of my soul."

Crane's coherence here lies in a consistent standard of values in which the Old Testament God is associated with cruelty, while the inner God is associated with love. Those who pursue the horizon "round and round" or seek the "rock" of truth share the standard of values represented by the "loud swagger" of the Old Testament God. Likewise, those who realize the "phantom" nature of truth and revere the individual conscience share the standard of values represented by the God who "whispers in the heart."

Chronology

1870

British South African Wars begin; Franco-Prussian War begins.

1871

Born on November 1 in Newark, New Jersey, to Jonathan Townley Crane, a Methodist minister, and Mary Helen Peck Crane, daughter of a clergyman; Stephen is the fourteenth and last child born to the couple; only eight of Stephen's siblings are alive at the time of his birth.

1874

First Impressionist exhibit in Paris.

1874–1882

Crane's father serves as a Methodist minister at churches in Bloomington, and then Paterson, New Jersey (scene of *Whilomville Stories*); mother is active in the Women's Christian Temperance Union; Stephen begins school; family moves to Port Jervis, New York, in April 1878; father dies on February 16, 1880, while pastor there.

1877

Queen Victoria is proclaimed empress of India.

1879

Thomas Edison invents first workable incandescent lightbulb.

1881

U.S. president James Garfield is assassinated.

1882

Indian chief Geronimo captured; Plains Indian warfare ends.

1883

Stephen's mother moves to Asbury Park, New Jersey, and writes articles for Methodist journals and newspapers;

Townley, Stephen's brother, operates a news reporting agency for *New York Tribune.*

1884

Berlin Conference decides European powers' spheres of influence in Africa; partition of Africa almost complete by 1895; Crane's sister, Agnes Elizabeth, dies at age twenty-eight.

1885

French chemist Louis Pasteur gives first inoculation against rabies.

1885–1887

Crane attends the Methodist boarding school Pennington Seminary.

1888

Crane enrolls in Claverack College and Hudson River Institute in January; in summers from 1888 to 1892, Crane assists brother in gathering news.

1890

Publishes first sketch, "Henry M. Stanley," as well as "Battalion Notes" column in the Claverack College *Vidette;* becomes first lieutenant in the school's military regiment; leaves Claverack after having only completed two and a half years of the four-year curriculum; enters Lafayette College in Easton, Pennsylvania, and joins Delta Upsilon fraternity, but completes only one term.

1891

Transfers to Syracuse University, where he plays catcher and shortstop for the varsity baseball team; works as a city correspondent for the *New York Tribune,* where his literary hoax, "Great Bugs in Onondaga," is published; publishes first short story in the *University Herald,* "The King's Favor," and writes first draft of *Maggie;* meets Hamlin Garland; goes on camping trip in Sullivan County, New York, with Frederic M. Lawrence, Louis E. Carr Jr., and Louis C. Senger Jr.; does not return to college; explores slums of lower Manhattan while living with brother Edmund in Lake View, New Jersey; mother dies.

1892

New York Tribune publishes several Sullivan County tales and sketches, as well as "The Broken-Down Van," though *Tribune* drops Crane after one of his articles offends a mechanics union. Moves to a roominghouse in Manhattan and shares a room with Frederic M. Lawrence; writes final version of *Maggie;* tours the Bowery.

1893

Stock market crash in June leads to a major economic depression; Crane self-publishes *Maggie: A Girl of the Streets;* begins *The Red Badge of Courage;* meets William Dean Howells; lives in an abandoned loft with friends; lives in poverty in several New York tenements.

1894

Writes "An Experiment in Misery," "In the Depths of a Coal Mine," and *George's Mother;* repeats camping trip with Carr and Senger in Pike County, Pennsylvania, after which he writes the "Pike County Puzzle"; sells *The Red Badge of Courage* to a newspaper syndicate owned by Irving Bacheller, which serializes the novel in newspapers.

1895

Bacheller sends Crane west and to Mexico to write material for his newspaper syndicate; first western sketch, "Nebraska's Bitter Fight for Life," is syndicated; *The Red Badge of Courage* published in book form, which results in Crane's fame both in the United States and in England; first volume of poetry, *The Black Riders*, is published; becomes a member of the Lantern Club, a group of journalists; spends summer with brother Edmund and writes *The Third Violet; Maggie* is reissued under Crane's name; goes to Florida to report on Cuba; meets Cora Howarth Taylor.

1896

George's Mother, another version of *Maggie*, and *The Little Regiment* are published; Crane visits Washington, joins Authors Club and becomes a member of the Sons of the American Revolution; back in New York, appears in court to defend prostitute Dora Clark and makes an enemy of the New York Police Department; goes to Florida to report on the Cuban insurrection.

1897

Greco-Turkish War over Crete; while enroute to Cuba aboard the *Commodore*, the ship sinks and Crane and three others spend thirty hours on the sea in a ten-foot dinghy; sails to Europe to cover Greco-Turkish War; Cora accompanies him and sends dispatches back under the name of Imogene Carter; returns to London; writes "The Monster," "Death and the Child," and "The Bride Comes to Yellow

Sky"; *The Third Violet* is published; Stephen and Cora settle in England; meets Joseph Conrad.

1898

Spanish-American War begins over Cuba, ends in same year with the Treaty of Paris, which gives Cuba independence and the United States the Spanish territories of Puerto Rico, Guam, and Philippines; United States annexes Hawaii; Crane attempts to join navy during Spanish-American War but is rejected; hired by Pulitzer to cover war in Cuba and Puerto Rico, where he reports on the landings at Guantanamo, the advance on Las Guasimas, and the Battle of San Juan Hill; *The Open Boat and Other Tales of Adventure* is published; writes "The Blue Hotel"; disappears in Havana for three months; returns to New York.

1899

Moves to Brede Place in England with Cora, where they struggle financially; *Whilomville Stories* and *Wounds in the Rain* are published; publishes second volume of verse, *War Is Kind,* as well as *Active Service,* and *George's Mother and Other Stories;* suffers hemorrhages from tuberculosis.

1900

Whilomville Stories, and *Wounds in the Rain* published; begins his last novel, *The O'Ruddy;* suffers hemorrhages; travels to Germany's Black Forest for his health; dies on June 5 of tuberculosis in a sanitarium in Germany; his body is returned to the United States for burial.

1901

Great Battles of the War published posthumously.

1902

Last Words, an anthology compiled by Cora, is published in England.

1903

Wright brothers make their historic first flight; *The O'Ruddy* is published.

FOR FURTHER RESEARCH

BOOKS BY CRANE

Stephen Crane, *The War Dispatches of Stephen Crane*. New York: New York University Press, 1964.

Stephen Crane, *Uncollected Writings*. Uppsala, Sweden: Uppsala University Press, 1963.

Wilson Follet, ed., *The Work of Stephen Crane*. 12 vols. New York: Russell & Russell, 1963.

Wilson Follet, ed., *The Collected Poems of Stephen Crane*. New York: Russell & Russell, 1930.

Donald J. Greiner and Ellen B. Greiner, eds., *The Notebook of Stephen Crane*. Charlottesville: The Bibliographical Society of the University of Virginia, 1969.

Thomas A. Gullason, ed., *The Complete Short Stories and Sketches of Stephen Crane*. Garden City, NY: Doubleday, 1967.

Joseph Katz, ed., *The Poems of Stephen Crane: A Critical Edition*. New York: Cooper Square, 1966.

Donald Pizer, ed., *The Red Badge of Courage: An Authoritative Text*. New York: W.W. Norton, 1994.

R.W. Stallman and Lillian Gilkes, eds., *Stephen Crane: Letters*. New York: New York University Press, 1960.

Stanley Wertheim and Paul Sorrentino, eds., *The Correspondence of Stephen Crane*. New York: Columbia University Press, 1988.

BIOGRAPHY

Thomas Beer, *Stephen Crane: A Study in American Letters*. New York: Octagon Books, 1972.

Christopher Benfey, *The Double Life of Stephen Crane*. New York: Knopf, 1992.

John Berryman, *Stephen Crane.* New York: Octagon Books, 1975.

Lillian Gilkes, *Cora Crane: A Biography of Mrs. Stephen Crane.* Bloomington: Indiana University Press, 1960.

Corwin K. Linson, *My Stephen Crane,* ed. Edwin H. Cady. Syracuse, NY: Syracuse University Press, 1958.

Eric Solomon, *Stephen Crane in England: A Portrait of the Artist.* Columbus: Ohio State University Press, 1964.

R.W. Stallman, *Stephen Crane: A Biography.* New York: George Braziller, 1968.

Stanley Wertheim, *The Crane Log: A Documentary Life of Stephen Crane, 1871–1900.* New York: G.K. Hall, 1994.

CRITICISM

Maurice Bassan, ed., *Stephen Crane: A Collection of Critical Essays.* Englewood Cliffs, NJ: Prentice-Hall, 1967.

Bert Bender, *Sea-Brothers: The Tradition of American Sea Fiction from* Moby-Dick *to the Present.* Philadelphia: University of Pennsylvania Press, 1988.

Harold Bloom, *Stephen Crane: Modern Critical Views.* New York: Chelsea House, 1987.

Joseph Conrad, *Last Essays.* London: J.M. Dent, 1926.

Linda H. Davis, "The Red Room, Stephen Crane, and Me," *American Scholar,* Spring 1995.

Ralph Ellison, *Shadow and Act.* New York: Random House, 1953.

Donald B. Gibson, *The Fiction of Stephen Crane.* Carbondale: Southern Illinois University Press, 1968.

Donald B. Gibson, The Red Badge of Courage: *Redefining the Hero.* Boston: G.K. Hall, 1988.

Thomas A. Gullason, ed., *Stephen Crane's Career: Perspectives and Evaluations.* New York: New York University Press, 1972.

David Halliburton, *The Color of the Sky: A Study of Stephen Crane.* Cambridge, England: Cambridge University Press, 1989.

Ernest Hemingway, ed., *Men at War: The Best War Stories of*

All Time. New York: Bramhall House, 1942.

Daniel Hoffman, *The Poetry of Stephen Crane.* New York: Columbia University Press, 1956.

Milne Holton, *Cylinder of Vision: The Fiction and Journalistic Writing of Stephen Crane.* Baton Rouge: Louisiana State University Press, 1972.

Claudia D. Johnson, *Understanding* The Red Badge of Courage: *A Student Casebook to Issues, Sources, and Historical Documents.* New York: Greenwood Press, 1998.

Giorgio Mariani, *Spectacular Narratives: Representations of Class and War in Stephen Crane and the American 1890s.* New York: P. Lang, 1992.

George Monteiro, "The Logic Beneath 'The Open Boat,'" *Georgia Review,* vol. 26, 1972.

Daniel K. Muhlestein, "Crane's *Open Boat,*" *Explicator,* Winter 1987.

Donald Pizer, ed., *Critical Essays on Stephen Crane's* The Red Badge of Courage. Boston: G.K. Hall, 1990.

Eric Solomon, *Stephen Crane: From Parody to Realism.* Cambridge, MA: Harvard University Press, 1966.

Robert Shulman, "*The Red Badge* and Social Violence: Crane's Myth of His America," *The Canadian Review of American Studies,* vol. 12, no. 1, Spring 1981.

R.W. Stallman, ed., *Stephen Crane: An Omnibus.* New York: Knopf, 1952.

Wallace Stegner, *The American Novel: From James Fenimore Cooper to William Faulkner.* New York: Basic Books, 1965.

Carl Van Doren, "Stephen Crane," *American Mercury,* vol. 1, 1924.

Richard M. Weatherford, ed., *Stephen Crane: The Critical Heritage.* London: Routledge & Kegan Paul, 1973.

Stanley Wertheim, *The Merrill Studies in* Maggie *and* George's Mother. Columbus, OH: Charles E. Merrill Publishing, 1970.

PERIODICALS

Stephen Crane Studies. Published at the Department of English at Virginia Polytechnic Institute and State University, Blacksburg, Virginia.

INDEX

8/05   5   4/05
5/16   10   3/14